Pierre Birot
Professor in the Sorbonne

The cycle of erosion in different climates

Translated by C. IAN JACKSON
Lecturer in Geography, London School of Economics
and Political Science

and KEITH M. CLAYTON
Dean of the School of Environmental Sciences
University of East Anglia

B. T. BATSFORD LTD London

First English Language Edition 1968
Reprinted 1969

Originally published in Rio de Janeiro
under the title *Le cycle d'érosion sous les différents climats*
© Centro de Pesquisas de Geografia do Brasil,
Faculdade Nacional de Filosofia, University of Brazil, 1960

Made and printed in Great Britain by William Clowes
and Sons Ltd, London and Beccles, for the publishers
B. T. BATSFORD LTD 4 Fitzhardinge Street, London W1
7134 2100 2

Contents

Translators' Preface

This book owes its origin to a series of lectures given in Brazil by Professor Birot after the Rio de Janeiro meeting of the International
Geographical Congress, 1956. A manuscript translation of the book
has been used in teaching for several years and has helped to remedy
the considerable shortage of work in English on the development of
landforms in the various climatic regions. This climato-morphology
has come to dominate continental European work, but despite the
earlier attempt by Peltier to formulate a general scheme of morphogenetic regions, the literature in English remains very limited. The
geomorphology that is taught in Britain is viewed as becoming increasingly conservative by continental workers, although this must
in part stem from an inadequate appreciation of the current literature. Conversely, many geomorphologists in Britain regard the
current continental predilection for identifying relics of earlier climatic régimes on the basis of landform alone, as of questionable
validity.

It seems to us that a particular attraction of Professor Birot's book
is that it represents the viewpoint of climato-morphology in a res-
trained and thoughtful manner, and seeks to relate it to the tradi-
tional (Davisian) outlook of the subject. By taking the best of what is
new, and the most tested and trusted of what is old, Professor Birot
has produced a geomorphology that will be found stimulating and
satisfying. He has thoroughly revised the original text for this
English translation, so that this is a fully up-to-date presentation of
the views of this most distinguished French geomorphologist. We are
delighted to thank him for all the work he has put into this new
version of his book. The diagrams have been redrawn by Mrs S. M.
Weston and Mrs Jeannemarie Stanton, and one new diagram has
been added. The bibliography has been brought up-to-date by
Professor Birot: it will be found a useful guide to the continental

literature, and an interesting commentary on the relative contribution
of English-language sources to the several chapters of the book. We
have conceived the translation as the communication of Professor
Birot's ideas to an English audience, so that the English text follows
the original French quite closely. However, terms such as *glacis* which
have no direct or simple connotation in English have not been rigorously translated by the same term throughout the book: instead
every effort has been made to convey to an English reader the sense
of the original in a terminology that he himself might use.

Despite repeated protestations to the contrary, international communication in geomorphology is at a low level, and all too few
geomorphologists overcome the barriers of language, terminology
and conceptual outlook that divide us. We hope that the translation
of this book may be a step in the right direction.

C.I.J.
K.M.C.

Introduction

The concept of a cycle of erosion expresses the evolution of slopes towards a level surface. Our purpose is to study this sequence of events in different climates.

At the outset it must be recognised that the term 'cycle' has itself been criticised. The word suggests an evolution that returns to its point of origin. But the Davisian 'cycle' begins with youth, passes through maturity and arrives at old age. It is hence an evolution that takes place in one direction only. Such criticism is certainly justified when one is dealing with the first cycle of erosion to affect a region, for example in the case of mountains which are geologically very young. However, the idea of a cycle is rigorously exact in all those cases where the area concerned has previously passed through senility, or even through the stage of 'maturity'. This is the case for the greater part of the land area of the world. All the ancient shields, all the folded mountain ranges of Mesozoic age (which are much more extensive than are Tertiary ranges), and even Tertiary ranges, have been planed at least once in their existence. We can suggest as an approximate, but fairly reliable, rule that any chain which was folded before the Miocene has already been base-levelled. One can therefore say that, over the greater part of the earth's surface, the landscape has at some time passed through old age; and that following this, renewed uplift has occurred, initiating new cycles.

The other fundamental objection currently made against the Davisian concept is the idea that in many cases orogenic movements and erosion have been contemporaneous and of roughly equal order of magnitude, so that the structures have been eroded *in statu nascendi*. But this is only important in areas of pronounced structural instability. Usually the earth movements come to an end, and then the cycle of erosion proceeds without having passed through the stage of youth in the sense in which we shall later define it.

In a first attempt to study the subject we shall begin in the middle of the evolutionary process (at the stage we may provisionally call maturity), by examining the simplest landscape which is possible. We are concerned, then, with a dendritic drainage pattern with interfluves which decline towards the streams.

The relief is composed of slopes of varying inclination. These slopes are generally convex in their upper part and concave in their lower part. They are covered by a layer of detritus, the thickness of which is approximately constant from top to bottom, and which is protected by a continuous plant cover. This may be herbaceous; more usually it is a tree cover with an undergrowth of herbaceous species. This is what one may call a 'normal' bioclimatic condition, and it implies a fairly humid climate. Obviously reservations may be made about this terminology; nevertheless it is the usual one and remains useful. We shall use the word 'soil' to describe this detrital cover; this is a useful convention and shorter than the alternative 'cover of detritus'. It is true that pedologists apply the term soil to the layer inhabited by organisms; thus in humid tropical regions it is relatively thin. This definition causes pedologists many problems because in fact they do not know at what level in the soil the action of life stops: microorganisms may appear well below the humus level. It seems preferable to treat the decomposed layer as a whole from the completely fresh rock up to the surface. This is in the interests of pedology as much as of geomorphology. The word 'soil', then, will be used for the detrital cover in the broad sense of the word.

The soil thickness also varies with the stage reached by the cycle of erosion. In the stage of maturity, which we are considering at present, its thickness is extremely variable, from a few decimetres in temperate regions, to several decametres in tropical regions. The further the cycle has progressed, the thicker the soil will be. The soil thickness expresses a balance sheet involving the rate of decomposition of the rock (the *Aufbereitung* of Walther Penck) and the speed of removal of debris on the slopes; these are the two processes which model the slope and which will be the subject of the following chapters. The presence of a soil immediately shows that this balance is positive and that its absolute value increases as the cycle of erosion progresses. Slopes will decline, and as the effectiveness of the agents of transport depends on the angle of slope, the thickness of the soil will increase as the rate of decomposition exceeds the speed of transport.

It must be added that as the slope declines, there will be a corresponding decrease in the speed of movement of water across it. The presence of water is an essential and indispensable factor in the decomposition of rocks; temperature changes alone are insufficient. Despite opinions to the contrary, water is the limiting factor in decomposition, even in humid tropical climates. An equilibrium is thus established in which climate affects both its elements, the rate of weathering and the speed of transport.

These agents of transportation move the debris as far as the river bed where, in the conditions of maturity, 'linear' erosion is concerned essentially with its removal. There is also erosion from the bed itself of previously weathered material, the thickness of which does not exceed that of the soil on the slopes. The profile of the bed is thus a provisional profile of equilibrium as described by H. Baulig. Its slope depends only upon the 'necessity' to remove the load provided by the slopes.

This concept of equilibrium allows for small oscillations which may be annual or more frequent, and which lead to temporary displacement on either side of the mean condition. If a catastrophic event occurs, for example the destruction of the forest cover by fire (which could well be a natural occurrence started by lightning), or a sudden landslip, there may be a very rapid increase in the alluvial load carried by the river. At first the discharge and slope of the river are unable to remove this increased load and temporary, localised deposition will occur. In subsequent years equilibrium will be re-established. By contrast, if we suppose an increase in discharge as the result of a particularly wet year without affecting the forest and so avoiding any appreciable increase in the amount of material supplied by the slopes, the ability of the stream to transport material will be increased, and the stream may incise itself a few decimetres, or even as much as a metre. Again this is a temporary oscillation, and the experience of European engineers in the control of rivers is that the bed of the stream does not alter. When the reasons for this stability of the river bed are investigated they are found to be twofold. In the first place it is the result of climatic oscillation on either side of a mean value. There is in addition a more fundamental cause for this stability, a type of automatic regulation of the régime. As in some other physical phenomena, any disturbance sets in train a series of events that tend to cancel its effects. Thus the compression of a gas causes heating which tends automatically to lead to expansion. We may suggest as an example a landslide, causing a section of forested slope to slip down and block the course of a river, so forming a lake on the upstream side. This initiates a series of changes that work to re-establish the profile of equilibrium: (1) alluvial material brought into the lake by the stream fills it, restoring surface flow; (2) headward erosion at the barrier takes place automatically; the slope here is steeper than before the slide and so the river will incise itself.

But a profile of equilibrium is only provisional. As the angle of slope decreases (an automatic result of any cessation of downcutting by the river), the load carried will decrease both in amount and in size. The stream will find itself to be underloaded; it will then cut down into previously decomposed rock, until the reduced slope (since the lower point at the river mouth is fixed) permits the stream to transport exactly the new load—a load increased to some extent as a result of the incision itself. Thus equilibrium is established again. Naturally this alluvial material must not be so thick that it exceeds the height difference between the river banks and the floor of the bed; otherwise deposition will occur. Outcropping of fresh rock, whether on the slopes or on the river bed, is a characteristic of youthfulness under these particular bioclimatic conditions.

To understand how the stage of maturity is reached, and how continuing evolution leads to senility, it is necessary to examine systematically the three fundamental processes, which are: (1) the decomposition of rock into detritus; (2) the transport of this detritus on slopes; and (3) the transport of this detritus in the river bed and the erosion of the river bed itself. So as to select homogeneous initial conditions, we shall mainly be concerned with a comparison of relief features developed on crystalline rocks.

PART ONE

The basic processes of the cycle of erosion

1 *The weathering of rocks*

It is possible to recognise two methods that can be used in the study of weathering processes; they are in many ways complementary to each other. The first method is the static or pedological approach. The profile from fresh rock to the soil surface shows a series of transitions, the size of the material of successive horizons becoming increasingly smaller towards the surface. Each horizon may be studied systematically. Granulometric analysis will give the distribution of the various fractions as a function of weight and this may be plotted on a graph. Petrographic analysis can be used to determine the proportion of fragments of fresh rock or minerals compared with those finer mineral fragments which have suffered chemical decomposition. Of these altered minerals, the gels and clays are particularly important. The gels are flocculated colloidal solutions, in which the constituent micelles are attracted towards each other although not assuming a crystalline state. The clays may also be colloidal in character, but show a microcrystalline structure. Comparison of successive horizons makes it possible to reconstruct the sequence of events in the weathering of the rock. This approach cannot give precise conclusions about the mechanisms involved; for example there are several explanations that might be used to account for the alteration of fresh granite, through kaolin, to laterite. Again, the normal sequence of horizons is likely to be disturbed in a soil developed on a slope. On the other hand, horizontal surfaces pose the difficulty that their soils are often polygenetic; in other words they have developed under a sequence of different climates.

There is consequently a need to employ the second method, the use of experiments. This consists of subjecting samples of fresh rock to different treatments in the laboratory: these may include alterations of temperature or of moisture, the action of various acid or alkaline waters, or of those carrying humus extracts. This experimental method has the advantage that it establishes the mechanism of rock decomposition. Nevertheless, there is the difficulty that even if the rock can be decomposed by subjecting it to conditions similar to those of the particular climate with which we are concerned, it cannot be certain that these processes are exactly those found under natural conditions. If, for example, granite is subjected to alternations of oven drying at a temperature of 70°C. and chilling in water at 20°C., this will cause some decomposition of the rock and the creation of a thin zone of alteration (*arène*). The climatic conditions which have been achieved in this experiment are those found in tropical regions with a long dry season; but we cannot be sure that the processes are exactly similar to those found under natural conditions where, for example, organic activity might be of importance. It must be remembered that there are problems of convergence, that is to say, similar effects may be the result of very different causes. It is important to use the static method, the approach of classical pedology, alongside that of experimental dynamics.

The factors of weathering

Before weathering processes can be classified, it is necessary to establish whether disintegration can occur without the presence of water. This is commonly accepted; disintegration as a result of temperature changes is often regarded as important even under completely dry conditions. These temperature changes are considered essential in granular disintegration, in rock shattering and in exfoliation.

Granular disintegration has often been attributed to the fact that the various minerals of a rock differ in conductivity, in their coefficients of expansion and in their ability to absorb heat; whether the rock forms by cooling (as in the case of granite) or by sedimentary cementation (as in sandstone). With these differences in their physical behaviour, the diurnal rise in temperature and resulting expansion of the minerals vary, and this is thought to lead to the loosening of the grains. However, both observation and experiments yield results which are unfavourable to this concept. In particular, examination of ancient monuments has shown that disintegration is at a maximum on the shaded walls of the monument (i.e. those that retain the most moisture) and not on the sides exposed to the sun. Laboratory experiments conducted by Griggs have been equally impressive. Granite fragments were exposed to 90,000 alternations of temperature of over 100°C. by rotating them in an apparatus that exposed them first to heat from an electric element, and then to a cooling current of fresh air. These pebbles remained completely intact and comparison of photographs taken before and after the experiment showed no trace of crystal fracture, or even any sign of cracks. The author's experiments (Birot, 1951, 1954) have led to the same conclusion; the alteration of granite implies the presence of water. It is true that temperature variations play a considerable role, but only because they increase the permeability of the rock, so aiding the penetration of water. This permeability can be measured by the speed of penetration of a colouring matter (such as methylene blue); the penetration has been tripled for rocks which have undergone a daily variation in temperature of over 70°C. over a period of four months. The conclusion is that it is impossible to continue to use the theory of granular disintegration in its original form (as used, for example, by B. Popoff to explain the existence of tafoni).

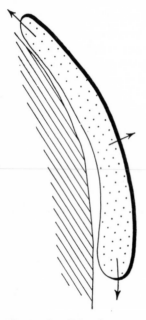

The problem arises in a still more complex form when the theory of thermal exfoliation is applied to homogeneous rocks. This invokes the contrast between the superficial rock slab which undergoes diurnal or annual variations in temperature and so expands and contracts, and the deeper part of the rock which shows practically no temperature variation. This is used to explain the development of a fracture and the detachment of a layer or scale from the rock surface. It is difficult to evaluate the worth of this theory, for as a result of the size of these slabs a controlled laboratory experiment is hardly possible.

Fig 1   Section of an exfoliation scale of which the internal part swells (the dotted section) while the outer part is covered with a veneer

The laws of thermodynamics enable us to be precise about the way in which these thermal variations occur, and the rate at which they decrease with depth. This rate is an exponential function. At a depth of two metres, the annual thermal variation (about 15°C. in the temperature zone) is reduced by one-half; at four metres it is scarcely a quarter of the surface value, one-eighth at six metres and so on. Diurnal oscillations penetrate less deeply: about one-twentieth of the annual oscillation. What is of importance when we consider the disruption of the rock, is clearly the gradient of the thermal oscillations as a function of depth; this is also exponential since the derivative of an exponential function is itself an exponential. For example, in the top 10 cm, the average gradient is 0.7°C. per cm, and falls to 0.3°C. in the next 10 cm. These values must be doubled for bare slopes. The result is that diurnal thermal oscillations are most likely to be effective in the upper layer, not exceeding a few centimetres in depth, while the annual oscillation may be felt through a metre of rock. In the intertropical zone, where the annual oscillation reaches a maximum of only 10°C., this last value must be still further reduced.

The preceding reasoning assumes that the rock surface is plane. In fact it is always more or less irregular, giving rise to convergence or divergence of thermal flow. The result of convergence is to perpetuate the curvature of the scales. On the other hand, Popoff has shown that concave surfaces undergo tension effects of longer duration than those on convex surfaces. In this case, in both the phase of contraction and that of expansion, the superficial layer tends to detach itself from the deeper rock which maintains a constant temperature (fig 2). In contrast, on a convex surface the scale will tend to detach itself only during expansion; contraction will merely create cracks perpendicular to the surface.

Are these theoretical possibilities found in practice? It is difficult to use laboratory experiments, for it would be unwise to reduce the size of the rock surfaces involved. It should be noted that the only examples of artificially induced exfoliation have been achieved with sandstone cobbles in the presence of more or less saline water (De Quesvain and Jenny, 1951). The only practical approach is through the study of exfoliation as a function of exposure. The sharpest thermal variations, and so the most effective, are produced on slopes that face the sun during the morning, or face towards the setting sun (making due allowance for cloud conditions.) In all cases these changes will be at a minimum on north-facing slopes in the Northern Hemisphere, and those facing south in the Southern Hemisphere. By contrast, if water is an important factor, these shaded slopes would be expected to undergo more rapid exfoliation. Although there are few sufficiently systematic observations on this subject, it seems that rapid exfoliation is most common on the shaded and moister slopes.

This approach has been used by J. Gentilli (1950) for the crystalline landforms of Australia. The degree of weathering was measured on all sides of large rock knobs. The maximum granular weathering (itself difficult to determine, it is true) takes place in the north-west

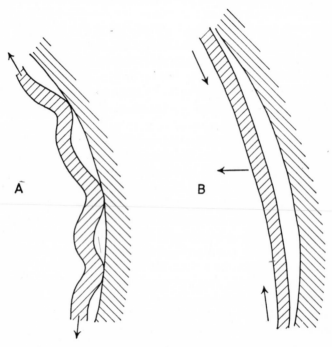

Fig 2   The effect of temperature variations on a concave face according to the concepts of Popoff. A—Expansion leading to corrugation of the surface layer. B—Contraction of the surface layer separating it from the rock mass

quadrant (two-thirds of the total amount). This might be explained by the fact that the maximum temperature variation is the result of the chilling of the face of the boulder heated towards the end of the afternoon (which by comparison with those sides exposed only to the morning sun, has received heat throughout the day). On the other hand, the more precise measurement of exfoliation (as distinct from granular weathering) has shown a more equal distribution by quadrants: south-east 21 per cent; north-east 22 per cent; north-west 20 per cent and south-west 37 per cent, so excluding any direct influence of variations in temperature. It would seem that, as in the case of granular weathering, the role of thermal changes is simply to assist the penetration of water to a constant depth below the surface.

The occurrence of pebbles of varying sizes which appear to have been split in two is often interpreted as a thermal effect. The break is clean and angular in contrast to the rounded contours of other surfaces. But experiments have shown that it is necessary to reach 200°C. to produce a fracture of this type. This suggests a natural fire resulting from lightning, while in desert regions the lightning flashes themselves might produce these fractures. In studying the remanent magnetism of old volcanic rocks, physicists have arrived at the conclusion that the frequency of lightning flashes capable of disturbing their remanent magnetism is considerable; so much so that only quarries offer sufficiently reliable samples for the determination of rock magnetism. On the other hand, similar fractures have been observed in huge rock knobs buried as much as five to six metres deep in tropical humid soils and so effectively insulated from temperature variations. The contrast between the rounded rock surfaces and the plane of the fracture can be explained either as the result of very different rates of weathering of an original rectangular joint pattern, so that the joint planes which are most readily weathered are converted into convex surfaces; or by an original joint pattern comprising both planar and convex elements.

We can now establish a classification of weathering processes based on the behaviour of water. Water may act in the solid form by causing shattering of the rock (congelifraction). But this process has a wide range of effectiveness varying from one rock to another, depending on the size of their pores. The most rapid effects result from the growth of an individual ice crystal by the migration of water contained within the soil. Where the pores are too small, water remains in the liquid state even when supercooled to very low temperatures. On the other hand, if the pores are too large and connected to the surface, water will be forced out as the ice crystallises.

In the liquid state water may work in a purely mechanical way. Insufficient attention has been devoted to the results of the expansion, with increase of temperature, of water contained in the pores of the rock; the coefficient of expansion is of the order of 10^{-3} compared with 10^{-6} for the minerals. It is also necessary to consider (as indicated by Strahler) the effect of the contraction during drying of the capillary films in the interstices of the rock, contractions which increase the pressure (inversely proportional to the radius of the drops) on the intervening grains. These two processes can be invoked to explain the negative results of a series of experiments, during which fragments of rock were alternately soaked in cold water, dried in a vacuum, and then placed in an oven at 70°C.; under these conditions no zone of alteration was formed.

There is, then, an almost continuous transition from physical-chemical phenomena to the true chemical dissociation of the molecule. A saturated solution, the volume of which is less than the sum of the crystal being formed from it and the remaining solution, is capable of creating a strong pressure on the walls of a cavity. In the same way, a growing crystal fed from a saturated solution possesses a considerable force of expansion which enables it, for example, to lift up a heavy object (40 kg/cm^2 for alum). The salts in question can be carried by the wind or be derived from the decomposition of the rock itself, which generally implies a previous purely chemical action.

A new crystal is capable of absorbing at its surface a certain quantity of water and this leads to an increase in volume. But these absorption phenomena are especially important in colloidal gels, such as silica gels[1] or iron gels, by virtue of the great size of their surface area in relation to their volume. The same phenomenon is produced between the laminae of clays and certain micas: montmorillonite possesses virtually explosive properties. For the process to be efficient, it is necessary for it to be capable of being repeated a large number of times, that is to say, after having undergone desiccation the substance must be capable of absorbing water again. This is the case for ferric gels when the desiccation takes place at low temperatures. But if the temperature is above 50°C., the phenomenon becomes irreversible, and the ferric oxide takes on the role of a cement rather than that of an explosive. In the case of hydration, water penetrates more deeply to the interior of the crystalline structure. For example, sodium carbonate can be transformed into a hydrate containing $7H_2O$, developing a pressure of 150 atmospheres. This is a third aspect of *Salzsprengung*.

By imperceptible transitions (at least in the case of silicates) we reach true chemical decomposition, which is in any case necessary to

---

[1] That these processes are efficient is suggested by the study of the crumbling of cements. An important factor is the formation of silica-soda gels from the siliceous debris in the mortar and the lime of the cement. This gel swells when it adsorbs water and so breaks up the cement (*Engineering Geology*, Geol. Soc. America, 1950, p. 225).

produce most of the 'explosive' changes already mentioned, with salts, clays and gels. In the case of calcareous rock, the laws of this chemical destruction, which simply consists of the formation of soluble bicarbonate, are sufficiently well known. Even water which is exactly neutral is capable of producing this alteration (about 13 milligrammes per litre). But this solubility is intensified by the presence of carbon dioxide. Depending on the quantity of this gas in the atmosphere, meteoric water is saturated to a greater or less extent (about 60 mg/litre for normal conditions of temperature and pressure). But at higher temperatures, this saturation is reached more rapidly, as is true of all chemical reactions.

By contrast, there is no agreement between chemists on the factors involved in the decomposition of complex silicas and sedimentary rocks derived from them. Silica in the form of quartz is much the most resistant element; in general it will only dissolve quickly in alkaline water (pH above 9). Felspars are aluminium silicates containing a variable quantity of potassium, sodium or calcium. The first stage of decomposition involves the solution of these alkaline elements which can occur even in neutral water. The disruption of the molecular structure only occurs much later; this implies a solution of the silica, which varies in importance according to the nature of the felspar and the type of decomposition. The mechanics of this disruption have been the subject of contradictory theories. For example, the action of neutral water on albite begins, according to Frederickson (1951), with the exchange of the sodium and hydrogen cations, while according to De Vore (1956), the agent of dissociation is the anion OH of water.

For a long time it was considered that clays are the result of the decomposition of felspars. Today, it seems that even the most simple clays (such as kaolin) which are aluminium silicates, represent the synthesis of silica and alumina: the alumina is completely dissociated at the expense of the felspars. These clays have a completely different laminar structure from that of the felspars. The nature of the clays produced varies, according to the relative proportions of silica and alumina present, as well as with the pH of the solution. These proportions themselves depend on the speed of movement of water through the rock. Although micas have a chemical composition which is more complex (for besides the silica and alumina and the alkaline metals, iron and magnesium are to be found), their laminar structure is analogous to that of clays, and the transition from one to the other is easier to understand.

The geomorphologist cannot ignore these purely chemical problems. On their solution depends an exact knowledge of the laws of differential erosion and of the influence of climate on the resistance to erosion of different rocks.

The plant cover is an essential agent in the decomposition of rocks. As soon as a rock is exposed to the atmosphere, for example after the retreat of glaciers, it is colonised by lower plants. First come algae and fungi, or more commonly lichens, which result from an association between the algae and the fungus. A first group includes superficial lichens which have at their base a cushion of fungi; slabs of even the hardest rock are covered by these lichens, giving a patina varying between grey and red. This cover forms acids which enable it to erode into even quartz or iron. Where the rock is more soluble, for instance limestone, the lichen encrusts them and rapidly extends towards the interior; the green of its chlorophyll appears when a stone is broken by a hammer blow. Each different type attacks a different rock. The sequence in which the minerals of granite are attacked is as follows: first biotite, then hornblende, then potassium felspars, and lastly quartz. When the rock has been decomposed to a depth of a few millimetres, the activity of the first lichens ceases, for they can no longer find the elements they need. They are succeeded by lichens of the second cycle, which have filaments that will penetrate several centimetres, even into the smallest fissures. Thus a residual siliceous microsol is created which is sufficient for the needs of mosses. These play an important role in chemical decomposition by virtue of the water reserves they hold (six times their weight) which may escape evaporation for as long as a week. After this stage, higher plants can establish themselves; these possess true roots, agents of rock destruction.

These roots can increase in size and exert a considerable mechanical pressure force, especially on the walls of joints and other cracks. At the same time, the roots behave as emitters of hydrogen ions which are exchanged for minerals necessary for the development of the plant, such as calcium. This vital function promotes the breakdown of calcareous and felspathic rocks. Sometimes a clay element performs an intermediary function (acid clay). The acid function of roots would be more important in the case of more primitive organisms.

The products of decomposition of plant material play a major role in rock breakdown, by modifying the pH of soil water. In general they increase its acidity by producing massive quantities of carbon dioxide and of organic acids of all types from acetic acid to lactic acid and the fulvic acids. This acidification of the soil water increases its aggressiveness in relation to calcareous and ferro-magnesian rocks, by dissolving the iron. In the attack on felspars, the presence of hydrogen ions can assist the removal of potassium, sodium and calcium, but in principle, this seems to be quite unsuitable for the removal of the silica and this constitutes a decisive phase; silica is known to be particularly soluble in alkaline water. However, complex acids such as aspartic acid seem particularly effective in desilification.

Here we must note also a vital difference between granitic (i.e. acidic) rocks on which organic and other acids have little effect (apart from a more rapid removal of calcium) and basic rocks on which the effect of organic acid is to increase the removal of silica anything from two to twenty times, at the same time as the removal of the basic cations (see the work of G. Pedro and M. Robert).

There is consequently the suspicion that soil bacteria play an important intermediary part in all these chemical reactions; a role whose importance cannot be underestimated, quite apart from the well-known action of fermentation with its release of large quantities of carbon dioxide. Some bacteria, using and regenerating small quantities of sulphuric acid, appear capable of beginning the laterisation of felspars. But tropical bacteria are still almost unknown and we are even more ignorant of their specific action on rocks.

Types of disintegration

The basis of the classification adopted here is the dominant size of the detritus produced.

GRANULAR DECOMPOSITION AND CLAY DECOMPOSITION The predominance of clayey or sandy decomposition depends on a number of factors. First of these is the nature of the rock. It is known that macrocrystalline or sandy rocks have a tendency to decompose into sand, while limestones (which include scattered insoluble impurities), microcrystalline rocks and schists (which are clay sediments) usually give clays. The nature of the climate is an almost equally important factor; in warm and wet climates, rapid chemical decomposition leads very quickly to the ultimate stage of decomposition, the production of clay. In contrast, in semi-arid climates, physical-chemical alteration only affects the cracks, and the intervening grains are removed without being appreciably broken down. Finally a very important factor is the relative speed of chemical decomposition compared with the speed of penetration of water. Where the rate of chemical alteration is rapid in comparison with the speed of penetration of water into the fresh rock, the superficial layer, which is saturated with water, is decomposed almost completely into clays before the water has appreciably penetrated into the interior of the fresh rock. This gives direct contact between the fresh rock and the clays. This is the type of soil section found on basic crystalline rocks, particularly in a humid tropical climate. By contrast, acid, coarse-grained rocks, especially when strongly fissured, have a broad zone of alteration between the clay particles at the surface and the fresh rock.

DECOMPOSITION INTO BOULDERS   Similar considerations may be used here. A necessary condition is the presence of joints through

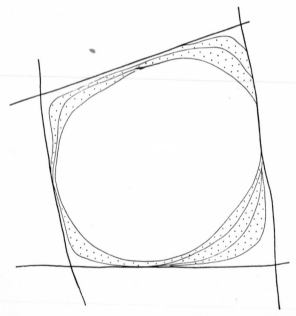

Fig 3   The evolution of a rounded boulder from a block formed by rectangular joints. Dotted areas indicate successive layers of decomposition

which water may readily penetrate, so that in the intervening zones, fragmentation into grains is almost non-existent. Thus physical-chemical decomposition progresses rapidly along these joints. The convergence of this rotting action transforms a cube-shaped rock into a rounded boulder (fig 3). But boulders of a rather similar type also appear pre-formed in the interior of the rock, where they are limited by curved fractures; the origin of these curved structures remains obscure. To distinguish between the two types of boulders it is necessary to examine deep sections that reach fresh rock. Boulders that originate from weathering and are still within the soil show a series of profiles, transitional between the original rectangular outline and the curved boulder surface. In contrast, 'primitive' boulders are enclosed only by a single curved fracture plane. It is not impossible, however, for structural boulders, formed as a result of unloading, to present a succession of curved surfaces which become more and more regular towards the centre.

DECOMPOSITION INTO FRAGMENTS   The predominance of fragmentation is the result of either a lithological factor (laminated rocks) or a climatic factor (periglacial frost shattering). In all cases, it is characteristic of a climatic environment where chemical action is relatively ineffective.

EXFOLIATION   In climates as varied as those of the Sahara, the Sierra Nevada of California and Rio de Janeiro, exfoliation forms the characteristic mode of decomposition, both of boulders and of rock monoliths with domed or sugar loaf form. It principally affects granitic or gneissic rock, but also sandstone or porphyry. The rock must be extremely resistant and normally fairly homogeneous. The rock can in fact be heterogeneous, provided the grains are fine. Those exfoliation scales which undoubtedly originate from subaerial weathering are never more than a few centimetres in thickness. They are covered on their external face with a veneer which may be siliceous or ferruginous. The principal signs of chemical decomposition generally appear on the internal face of the scale (fig 1).

This process seems to be explained in the following way. In rocks which are sufficiently homogeneous, temperature variations penetrate to a constant depth below the surface of the ground (though this depth will increase a little in zones of convergent thermal flow). These variations of temperature increase the permeability of the rock by opening up minute fissures in the grains. In all climates, a bare rock with a steep slope will retain moisture for only a short time, particularly at the surface. But at a depth of a few centimetres, water persists longer and initiates clayey decomposition, leading to swelling of the interior section. At the same time ferro-silicic solutions are drawn to the surface by capillary action where they precipitate to give a veneer that is particularly well-developed in semi-arid climates. The increase in volume resulting from the clayey decompositions leads to the detaching of the scale. The scale will only remain intact if the rock is resistant to granular disintegration; that is to say, where it is poorly fissured and of fine grain.

The occurrence of layers of scales of unequal thickness can be the result of annual and diurnal temperature variations. It is also necessary to envisage a series of scales parallel to curved joint surfaces, which are not necessarily of subaerial origin. Water circulates more readily in these zones of weakness where the rock is in a state of tension, and premature chemical decomposition initiates the separation of layers several metres thick. The origin of these curved joints is, however, a mystery.

2 The transport of debris on slopes

Here, again, it is possible to use a direct and an indirect approach. The direct method consists of field observation of the moving detritus, although this is normally only possible for rapid movements. Thus the wash produced by a violent rainstorm can be examined. This would show the maximum size of debris carried by this process and whether the material consisted largely of sand grains or fine gravel. This information should be supplemented by meteorological records from the nearest station of the amount of rainfall that particular day. This will give the competence of the wash to transport debris of a certain size on a particular measured slope, despite the presence of a plant cover, whose continuity must also be noted. Similar studies can equally well be made of certain slower phenomena, for example pipkrakes (fig 4). This involves ice needles which, as they grow, raise a grain of sand or other piece of debris at right-angles to the slope; the ice then melts, and the grain of sand falls to a position a little lower down the slope. This phenomenon can be observed during the course of a frosty winter day in temperate regions.

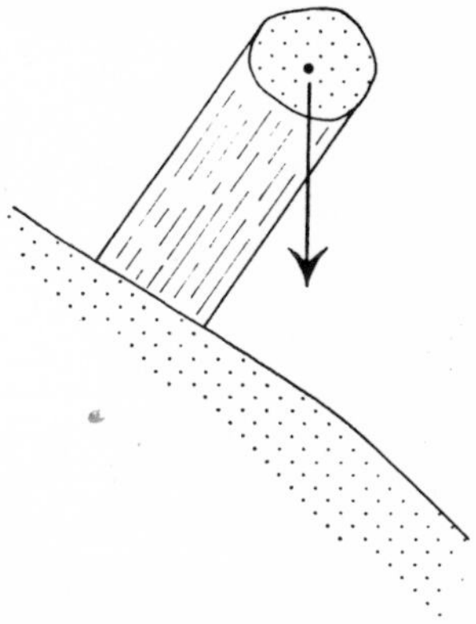

Fig 4 Mechanics of a pipkrake. A needle of ice lifts a spherical grain away from the surface: when the ice melts the grain should fall a little way down the slope

For the majority of slow movements, it is necessary to use indirect methods. That is to say, the material which has been moved from a particular position over a long period of time may be identified in soil sections. The lithological elements which are particularly resistant to

decomposition are noted, and when they can be easily identified
within the soil they can be traced from their point of origin to the bottom of the slope, as for example where fragments are derived from a
quartz vein (fig 5, *top*). If the size of this material is measured
throughout the length of the slope, it will give a law of the reduction

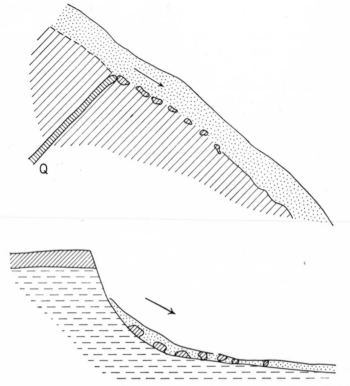

Fig 5   *Above*, Slow sliding of debris on a slope away from a vein of
quartz. *Below*, Sliding of debris from a band of resistant rock
(shaded) from a cornice formed by the rock band. Fine material is
stippled

of size of the particles as a function of distance from the vein, for a
particular plant cover, etc. Another very general case where this
method may be applied is where a slope is capped by a resistant bed
(for example a hard sandstone), that can be clearly distinguished
from the marls or soft schists found below (fig 5, *bottom*). By examining the soils throughout the length of the slope, fragments of sand-

stone may be found, their size decreasing downslope, and it is possible
to establish the law of diminution of size as a function of distance for a
given slope. This reduction is the result either of sorting or of wear
suffered during transport. In the latter case the rate of diminution of
size expresses the relation between the speed of reduction, as a function of time, and the speed of transport. As we shall see, the problem
is exactly the same as that encountered when studying the alluvial
material of a river bed. It is no less important to follow the course of
the detritus from a simple rock of average resistance. For this one can
choose a slope where successive, and roughly equal, outcrops of two
or three rocks of this type occur (for example schists and granites),
the detritus from which may be readily recognised, even after considerable alteration.

An experimental approach may also be used, but it is much less
helpful than the study of rock decomposition. With a simple inclined
plane it is possible to study the stability of various materials as a function of slope. For example, the angle of rest of unsorted rubble has
been found by civil engineers to be about 35°. As for other phenomena, it may be said that there are no systematic studies in this field,
apart from the work in progress at Strasbourg on the experimental
study of flow.

Different types of transport

The resistance of fragmented material to movement is in part due to
its cohesion and in part to the friction exerted by different parts on
each other and on the rock below. Unlike cohesion, friction increases
according to the weight of the overlying material. Cohesion, in its
simplest form, is due to the attraction exerted by very thin films of
water; it is virtually nil in the case of particles larger than two mm.
In the case of true soils, the fragments are also held together by colloids or chemical precipitates. In alluvial soils, and in particular in
clays, cohesiveness is the primary factor preventing movement. Above
a particular value of moisture content, about 10 per cent for clays,
movement en masse can take place, up to a water content of 80–90
per cent. With even higher water content, the material will move as a
fluid, cohesion falling to zero.

In the general case, equilibrium conditions are defined by
Coulomb's equation:

$$s = \sigma \tan \rho + c$$

where

    s = shear stress along the shear plane between the particles,
    σ = pressure at right-angles to this plane,
    ρ = the angle of internal friction,
    c = cohesion.

The methods of transport can be classified on the basis of three features: (1) the speed of movement; (2) the degree of coherence of the debris being moved; and (3) whether the debris is carried along by an agent, or simply moves under the influence of gravity. This last distinction is very important; the material may move as a result of the gravitational forces acting on it due to its position on a slope, or it may be carried along by water or occasionally even by wind or ice.

Wash

Wash affects individual fragments of detritus and works at a speed that is infinitely greater than the speed of rock decomposition. Naturally the size of material moved depends to a considerable extent on the climate and on the plant cover; in general the smaller detritus is involved, of the size of sands or even of silts. For material the size of gravels, wash is less efficient, except in certain semi-arid climates. Wash is therefore a selective method of transport, in contrast to other processes which carry all the available material regardless of size. It moves detritus which is thoroughly weathered and as a result is a significant agent of differential erosion. It rapidly attacks those rocks which decompose almost directly into fine detritus the size of sand or smaller, but does not affect those rocks that break down into fragments of greater size. By comparison with other agents of transport on slopes, wash is still relatively efficient even on a slope of only 1°. Thus, even though it is only able to carry small fragments, it can do this over very gentle slopes; this is vital in understanding the laws of the evolution of slopes in arid climates, as we shall see later. One factor which does limit the activity of wash is a plant cover. Where this cover is continuous—as for example in grassland (the plants touching each other at their bases)—or in a temperate forest where the ground layer is equally continuous, wash has very little effect. The water is obstructed by the stems, and a layer of plant litter protects the underlying soil. Only plant detritus can be carried away by the wash; in this respect it is no more active than ants. The layer with which we are concerned, the mineral soil beneath, is untouched, and so the slope is virtually unaffected. In a humid tropical forest (such as that of the Ivory Coast), the ground flora under primary rain forest is much less continuous than in temperate forest, and it appears from careful observations made by Rougerie that under these conditions wash can move very fine sands and especially silts. Ruellan also believes that wash is of significance under tropical rain forest. In secondary forest, which has a better developed shrub layer than primary forest, it seems that the effectiveness of wash must be similar to that under temperate forest. By contrast, in arid climates where the plant cover is discontinuous, wash is all important. It is the main agent of transport, carrying material up to the size of gravel and shingle. The quantity of plant matter here is very small and consequently the organic layer of material, such as partially decomposed leaves, is non-existent or very discontinuous; here wash freely erodes the mineral soil and not merely the organic layer. The presence of a deep humus layer has another disadvantage from the point of view of wash: it is very permeable. The slope is covered by a layer of matted plant remains and the water, instead of flowing across it, infiltrates into it. At times this may lead to a sub-surface movement capable of initiating erosion.

Avalanches should be placed in the same category.

Landslips

Those detrital movements which do not result from the transport effect of an external agent will next be considered. In these cases it is often found that only when water soaks into the debris does movement occur.

Landslips form a major category in which the motive force is gravity, acting on the debris itself. In the case of landslips the resulting movement is abrupt and rapid. In this way they may be distinguished from other movements brought about by gravity. These landslips always occur on steep slopes, and the material affected may be of very great size. It is necessary to distinguish between rockfalls building talus cones or screes on the one hand and landslides on the other. Screes result from individual movements; landslides move in one piece. Talus is derived from rock *in situ*, whether granite or sandstone grit. Landslides and other smaller movements may take place either at the expense of unconsolidated rock *in situ* (sand, clay, etc.) or at the expense of a thick soil, itself derived from the rock beneath.

Talus results from the action of gravity on a particularly steep slope. Let us suppose such a steep slope, where joints are to be found at all inclinations. The rock *in situ* is consequently broken into a series of blocks. If the slope is greater than the equilibrium slope of these blocks, they will slide one over the other along the inclined joints. The momentum they acquire allows them to travel across a more gentle slope than that on which the movement first occurred. The momentum is proportional to the diameter, so that it is the largest blocks which travel the farthest. At the end of their travel they may collide and rebound. As a general rule talus occurs in dry conditions; however, the movement of the blocks is made easier if chemical decomposition exploits the joints and lubricates the slip planes. The formation of ice wedges leads to the same results.

When the slope is greater than 60°, even when it is developed on very compact rocks, such erosion phenomena tend to occur even in the absence of joints. Moreover a normal fault with an angle of exactly 60° is often no more than a large-scale slip, the rock breaking because it cannot support this strain.

By contrast, landslips or landslides affect unconsolidated rocks or very thick soils. This loose material is subject to shearing, either along a curved surface if it is very thick, or along the plane of contact with the fresh rock. The critical thickness in the first case is:

$$d = \frac{c}{g\gamma} \cdot \frac{1}{\sin \alpha - \tan \rho \cos \alpha}$$

where γ is the density, α the angle of slope, $\tan \rho$ the angle of internal friction. A necessary condition is that α is greater than ρ.

The saturation of a layer of soil by water leads to the creation of an upward hydrostatic pressure which affects its stability. A new arrangement of particles then becomes possible which leads to the liquefaction of the whole mass. At the surface this forms a scar which is often seen in areas that have suffered erosion as a result of human activity, for example in recently deforested areas such as the Paraiba valley, on clay or sandy land resulting from the decomposition of granite. Even under forest in a warm and moist climate, soils which result from the decomposition of even the hardest rocks, slump periodically on slopes steeper than 45° (as shown, for example, by the extremely precise work of Wentworth and White in Hawaii). Landslides are also found in dry regions, but here they affect solid rock, provided that it is composed of saline clays. At the end of an exceptional rainstorm, the clay is saturated and in the presence of salts of a suitable type the colloids deflocculate; when this happens, slope failure will occur.

Flow, creep and saltation

All the phenomena dealt with in the previous section are rapid, whether they take the form of wash or landslips. We now turn to the slow phenomena, affecting the whole depth of the soil (or at least a considerable proportion of it), which may be grouped under the term flow. The speed of flow is of the order of a few metres per year at a maximum. The soil behaves as a plastic mass which above a certain load moves as a very viscous fluid, the speed of the upper layers being the greatest with a decline in velocity towards the base, following the laws of laminar flow. Shear stresses well below those which cause slipping are sufficient to cause plastic deformation when applied over a very long time.

The factors which weaken cohesion are: (1) an excess of water which peptises the colloids, dissolves the precipitates holding the grains together, and decreases the forces of attraction between them; (2) ice, which disturbs the soil aggregates; (3) the mechanical activity of burrowing animals. The angle of internal friction is reduced by the increase of pore space through chemical solution and the removal of colloids.

What are the factors determining whether the material will move by flowing or by slipping? Slope is one of the most important factors; landslips are only produced on very steep slopes (more than 40°), while periglacial solifluction may occur on slopes of a few degrees. The climatic régime must also be taken into account; a constantly humid climate favours flow, while sudden, heavy showers (provided they fall on soil which is already saturated) are usually responsible for landslips. Finally a more difficult factor to establish is the texture of the soil and the nature of the clays and colloidal gels which enter into its composition. Sandy soils saturated with water are likely to slip (as has been found by every young child building sandcastles on the beach); by contrast a predominance of clays and silts assists flow, particularly because only a very small quantity of water is needed to saturate them. Thixotropic bodies are naturally subject to sudden slips, while clays belonging to the kaolin group move slowly. Plastic movement affects soil where silica and hydroxides of iron remain mobile (*Lehm* in Kubiena's terminology) in contrast to *Erde* where the colloids are irreversibly precipitated and held in aggregates. Flow is produced in many climates: humid temperate, humid tropical, periglacial, etc.

It is convenient to group under the heading 'creep' all the ways in which particles are moved without the assistance of an external fluid, and where the average free travel does not exceed a few centimetres. This phenomenon may be caused by any factor capable of making a particle change its position. Gravity is dominant because the balance of any such movement will lead to a net downward displacement. The displacement may be caused by a needle of ice raising a particle perpendicular to the slope; the melting of the needle allows the particle to fall vertically with net displacement of a few centimetres (fig 4). Showers of heavy rain will disturb the ground surface, throwing particles in all directions, but here again the net movement will be down slope. The amount of movement is particularly great where the mineral particles are raised high above the slope by the tearing out of the roots of a falling tree. Disturbance by animals is particularly important where the plant cover is dense and continuous; mineral fragments thrown out by burrowing rodents fall down the slope. Taking the concept to its logical conclusion, we might even include those regions in southern Africa where monkeys throw stones at each other. But all these phenomena are best considered as a form of saltation.

Certain movements fall into an intermediate category between creep and flow. This is the case where the movement affects a mass of fine detritus of which the elements are all displaced at much the same time: silts alternatively soaked and dried in a dry climate, or undergoing freeze-thaw in a periglacial climate. In arid climates it is possible to envisage thermal creep, demonstrated in the laboratory for almost a century. A plate, placed on an inclined plane and subject to alternating heat and cold, will move towards the base of the slope. One can put in the same intermediate category the settling, sometimes individual, sometimes collective, which affects the superficial layers of a soil where dissolved material is being carried away by the percolating water. It is to movements of this type that the term 'creep' is best confined.

Finally it must be noted that weathering of rock is not of itself enough to render detritus mobile. In all slope sections it is important to distinguish carefully between the fixed part where the products of decomposition (excluding those carried away in solution) do not suffer any movement, and the colluvial layer. In practice this distinction is not always easy. The presence of veins which are resistant to weathering forms the best guide. In the same way, below an illuvial crust, the soil may be considered immobile, precipitation of iron and calcium having the effect of paralysing it. However, one must not forget that part of the soil may be immobile for a long period only to be carried away by some sudden landslide.

The decomposed material can only be distinguished from the fresh rock by some arbitrary criterion, such as whether or not it is deformed by compression of a particular amount.

Quantitative study of the loss of material from slopes

One of the most difficult tasks, but also one of the most useful, is the quantitative measurement of the loss of material from slopes. The slope selected must have a simple geometric form, and in particular must carry a vegetation cover that is as similar as possible to the natural cover.

i Rapid superficial movements. Transport by wash and solution belongs in this category. To collect the water involved in wash together with its load it is necessary to dig a ditch some 10–20 cm in depth, following a contour. The trench must have a wall of thick cement on its upslope side so that artificial flow cannot occur. The trench leads the water into troughs with a volume of three or four m³, depending on the duration of the experiment and the time interval between measurements. The sand, silt and clay can be collected and the water analysed to give the quantity and type of material transported in either true or colloidal solution. For the big slopes of the *morros* of Rio, the necessary drainage channels already exist. This method has been used in more difficult conditions than those of Rio: in French Guinea and the Ivory Coast. It has been possible to measure both the intensity of surface wash and the amount of material carried in chemical solution.

In order to measure the quantity of dissolved products, not only in surface water, but also in the water that percolates through the soil, a series of openings, too small to allow any soil to be washed through, must be made in the cement wall at the head of the trench, transforming the wall into a type of filter. From the experiments of Freise in Brazil, it seems that the greater part of the debris transported in chemical solution is contained in these infiltrating waters. Particularly in a dry climate, one of the most important problems is the determination of the maximum size of the material transported by surface wash (competence of the wash). For this coloured fragments of quartz must be placed on the surface of the slope under study; these have the advantage of having the same density as the natural rock. Where it is possible to work in a scientific reserve or some similar protected experimental area, violent colours that are easily seen can be used. However, in an area used by farmers who might disturb an experiment it is better to use fragments of some natural rock not found on the slope under study, for example, quartz on a slope of limestone and marls. The study of talus uses similar methods. They have been successfully applied in northern Scandinavia where the annual volume of stones falling from a valley side has been measured.

2   More difficult to study are movements such as creep and flow. The best way is to place coloured, indestructible debris at various depths within the soil profile. Naturally their precise initial position must be known, and for this it is necessary to build across the slope a barrier of some material resistant to chemical change, and extending to a sufficient depth to be unaffected by the soil movement. After some years, the particles are re-located and their movement measured. This method has been used in the French Alps to study the effects of flow. Obviously it is impossible to distinguish between the movement due to creep and that due to flow.

3   A third type of technique attempts to get a generalised picture of the surface effects of erosion. A precise profile of the surface of the slope is levelled and this can be compared with a similar profile measured at a later date. The change in the profile will be the result of very different processes; not only superficial erosion by creep, or wash, but also effects of subsidence induced by flow or percolating water. Another comprehensive method consists in taking photographs of a particular slope, and comparing these with other photographs available for other years. From these it may be possible to list all the changes that have taken place in the position of superficial pebbles, small irregularities in the ground surface and so on. This has been done in widely differing areas: for example in the Grand Canyon of Colorado, two photographs taken at an interval of 60 years have enabled us to conclude that on one section of slope there has apparently been no change at all. A second example of this method,

the subject of a paper at the Rio Congress, was concerned with talus slopes on Spitzbergen. Photographs taken at an interval of 50 years have shown that several blocks of very large size have not undergone any disintegration, and the point of impact of their fall is still visible. In contrast, on the slopes of the Ivory Coast, photographs taken by Rougerie at only a few years' interval have shown important changes: the lowering of small crests, the infilling of small depressions.

The slowness of erosion is such that it is normally necessary to use even more general methods of studying a slope where it is possible to give a precise date to an old surface which is incompletely destroyed, so that the volume of material removed by erosion may be estimated. In the northern Sahara, for example, the greater part of a slope in siliceous rock is covered with a shiny veneer composed of silica, iron and manganese. Archaeological evidence suggests that this was formed 5,000 or 6,000 years ago; this is suggested by primitive rock drawings depicting the animal life of a Neolithic Sahara. The veneer has been lost by exfoliation, generally at the base of granite inselbergs, to a depth of the order of one or two centimetres. Inspection of the inselbergs gives the proportion of surface occupied by veneer and by bare areas. On 'rhyolitic' inselbergs there has been no loss of material. On granites the ratio of scar to veneer is about 1 : 20 (1 : 10 in certain cases); that is to say the average thickness removed is about one-twentieth of one cm, of the order of 0.05 mm. The same technique may be used where a rock surface has been polished by the passage of ice, and is in course of destruction by post-glacial weathering. In valleys in the central Pyrenees this demonstrates that congelifraction occurred during a relatively dry periglacial phase that followed the retreat of the local glaciers.

Contradictory opinions have been expressed on the speed of erosion of the sugar loaves of Rio de Janeiro. These doubts could be settled by systematic study of the lichen-covered surfaces and of those parts which are bare and represent the weathering of the surface or the recent fall of material. If we know the time taken by lichens to spread over a square metre of fresh surface it is possible to derive some idea of the approximate speed of present erosion, on the basis of the proportion of the total surface so far uncolonised by lichens (which is very small).

Finally the most general of all methods used to attempt to evaluate the amount of material lost from slopes is to measure the load carried by the rivers that drain an area. The total load is divided by the area of the basin to give the loss of material per unit area. This measurement must be made over several years, for even in a region devoid of extremes there are annual variations, so that in some years the rivers carry away more than they receive from the slopes and sometimes less. Following a landslip a considerable quantity of detritus will arrive at the foot of a slope, but the river will only be able to move a small part of this; only after several years will all the materials have been washed away. It is best to choose a drainage basin of fairly small size with more chance of homogeneity in rock types so that the various factors affecting the transport of debris on the slopes can be studied separately; the angle of slope is the most important of these. A large basin will always include steep slopes in its higher reaches and more gentle ones in the lowland areas. For practical reasons measurements so far available are for sizeable rivers but a serious difficulty, making them of little value, is that they include large areas disturbed by man. What is needed is a study of a small drainage basin of about 100 acres in conditions such as those in the Itatiaia National Park, where the vegetation, although not original, has been re-established and where the slopes are all on syenite.

Finally even the measurement of the material transported by the river encounters serious technical difficulties. It is quite easy to measure the transport by solution or suspension; a bottle is plunged into the river and the water evaporated before or after filtering, enabling the separation of solution and suspension. The great difficulty is to measure the traction load and even able scientists with elaborate apparatus have not found a way. If a trap is placed on the bed of the river, in an attempt to collect the alluvial load carried along by the stream, eddies are caused and the resulting turbulence destroys the natural conditions, making it impossible to tell whether the material trapped is greater or less than the natural quantity. This is a common problem in science where the process of measurement disturbs the object one is attempting to measure. Only the measurement of material accumulated behind a dam will give a true picture of the material transported by a river. From time to time when such a dam is drained, it is possible to examine the material that has accumulated: an excellent opportunity to examine the size and chemical composition of the river's load.

3 Fluvial dynamics

The object of this chapter is not to study the whole of fluvial dynamics for its own sake, but to investigate two or three very general
features which are fundamental to the theory of the cycle of erosion,
and in understanding the form of slopes. Among these features the
most important is undoubtedly the general concavity of the longitudinal profile of equilibrium. In reality this curve is not continuous,
and would be only if the discharge increased smoothly down the
stream, which is roughly true for a river without major tributaries.
Usually the profile is broken up into a series of segments of gradually
decreasing steepness, with a break of slope at each important confluence. The load carried increases at the same time, in almost the
same proportion, for it is a function of the area of the basin. Thus the
problem is to understand how the river is capable of transporting
this increasing load of solid material although the slope of the river
becomes more and more gentle.[1] Two particular factors may be
significant here, a specifically hydraulic factor, an increase in the transporting efficiency of the stream with increased discharge, and the
decrease in size of the alluvial material downstream. But before considering the first of these, it must be remembered that as well as
examining the longitudinal profile of equilibrium, we must also take
the cross-profile of the wetted section into account. In the same way
that the longitudinal profile develops equilibrium by a series of automatic adjustments, so does the cross-profile, and it is in vain to seek a
law controlling the longitudinal profile without at the same time including the variation in the cross-section of the bed.[2] Thus in the

[1] In a series of very important papers, Luna Leopold and his associates have
shown that *the most probable* form is a concave profile. But the processes which lead
to its development have still to be investigated fully.

[2] This is one of the reasons why Chapter 1 of an earlier work, *Essai sur quelques
problèmes de morphologie générale*, Lisbon 1949, must be considered as partially out of
date.

majority of the formulae, the transporting capacity of the river is expressed as a function of the width of the bed. Even in the smallest streams, the flow is turbulent. If the motion of the water were laminar, with successive layers of water sliding over one another rather like a pack of cards, there would be very little erosion of the river bed, even though the surface water would be moving with the speed of a bullet. The flow is in fact turbulent, the different layers mixing with one another by the random exchange of molecules. Some molecules move from the rapid layer towards a slower layer, so speeding it up; other molecules move from the slower layer towards the more rapid layer, so slowing it down; as a result the general flow of all the water in the river is homogeneous. These exchanges function simultaneously at all scales up to immense waves of several metres in diameter. It is because the quickly moving surface layers tend to transmit their speed to even the lowest layers of the water that erosion of the bed can occur.

The speed of the water at the river bed is the essential factor of fluvial action; the total transporting capacity of the river, the limit to the size of material it can move and its ability to erode the rock *in situ* are all related to this figure. The average speed of the water is fairly well known both from field observation and experiment provided that there is no transport at the bed of the stream and the water is clear. This average speed is a function of the slope I and the hydraulic radius R; it varies as $V = KR^{2/3} I^{1/2}$ (the hydraulic radius is the ratio between the wetted section S and the wetted perimeter). In a river which is much wider than deep, which is the usual case with very large rivers (for example 500 metres wide and 10 metres deep), the hydraulic radius is approximately equal to the depth, so that the depth is more significant than the slope of the river. Significant evidence for this is that along the length of a stream which is in equilibrium, the average speed varies only slightly from source to mouth. But the essential factor for erosion is the speed at the base of the stream; the ratio between the average speed and the bed speed has been determined in pipes and in flumes (in clear water). In turbulent flow, the fundamental relationship is $V = C \sqrt{IR} (8.48 + 5.75 \log \Upsilon/d)$ where Υ is the distance from the base of the bed and d expresses the roughness diameter at the base of the bed (in the case of the profile of equilibrium, the pebbles at the base of the bed). This series of formulae enables the calculation of the speed at the bed of the river, given the slope, the wetted section and the discharge of the river, and the diameter of the alluvial material. To be strictly accurate, these formulae are only valid where there is no transport. Where the material at the base of the river is moved, the kinetic energy absorbed by this interaction may be divided into two parts: (a) useless turbulent agitation which reduces the average speed of the river and is finally dissipated in heat, and (b) energy transformed into useful work, that is to say the movement of alluvial material.

Various attempts have been made to express the ability and capacity for total transport of rivers, on the basis of a mixture of theoretical calculations and experiments. The two principal methods of transport of material must be examined separately: transport in suspension and transport on the bed (traction load). Transport in suspension is a result of the turbulence of the fluid. It affects very fine particles which are carried in ascending turbulent currents. When they encounter negative turbulent currents, they descend, and so describe a type of sinusoidal motion. In each section of water, the ascending currents raise a certain percentage of suspended matter to the layer above, so giving a logarithmic vertical distribution. Given the slope I, the hydraulic radius R, etc., the quantity of material that can be carried in suspension can be calculated accurately. But this formula is of limited value, for most rivers are very far from saturation with suspended material. In general, this is not a limiting factor in the determination of the profile of equilibrium. There are a few exceptions to this, such as the rivers of the loess region of northern China; these have much more fine material available than is usual and may at times carry loads of up to half the weight of the water, with all stages of transition to what is effectively a mud-flow. In all other cases, wash does not supply such large quantities of material to the river.

The traction load is the critical factor which determines the load carried by the river, and determines its longitudinal and cross-profiles of equilibrium. Pebbles progress by irregular movements by rolling around their principal axis of symmetry. The bed itself does not slope regularly downstream, but includes raised bars (riffles) and pools. The first are constructed by the finer material, and the larger material is found in the hollows. These bars generally have an asymmetrical form similar to dunes. The traction load climbs an inclined ramp and then descends the downstream side; the bar as a whole tends to move in a downstream direction, just as do dunes in the path of the wind. The pebbles are raised by ascending turbulent currents which are themselves dependent upon the vertical gradient of speed. The difference in the speed of adjacent layers of the water leads to hydraulic lift.

Particles are raised where the speed of the water is greatest, then they slide down into the next hollow. The variations in turbulence give a series of successive impulses so that the pebble advances by fits and starts.

When the energy imparted by the hydraulic lift exceeds a certain value, the particle detaches itself from the bed and follows a trajectory through the water, being carried forward by the movement of the upper water layers before falling down again. This process of saltation is, however, much less important than the others. The haphazard fluctuations that characterise hydraulic lift explain the limitations of all the attempts to provide a simple formula to express the competence of a river. The formula

$$K\left(\frac{d}{R}\right)^{1/6} = \frac{RI}{d}$$

(d being the maximum diameter of the material being carried) is only approximate. A further difficulty derives from the fact that the critical conditions for removal are not the same for a single particle as for a group of particles (R. Bagnold). A mass of detritus is only set in motion by a force much greater than that needed to move a single fragment of the same size.

As for the determination of the total weight of material transported (the capacity), this clearly involves still more complex factors. An attempt at this is the formula of Meyer-Peter, where the slope varies between 0.4 and 23 per 1,000 and a grain diameter between 0.4 and 28 mm. The formula is

$$G_1 = \left[\frac{Q_s}{Q}\left(\frac{K_s}{K_r}\right)^{3/2} IH - Bdm\right]^{3/2}$$

G_1 represents the solid load per metre of width of the bed, Q_s a hypothetical discharge the calculation of which enables the influence of the banks to be eliminated, Q the actual discharge; but this is only a very rough approximation, for it assumes uniform distribution of speed throughout the section. K_r is the coefficient of roughness of the bed, depending only on the diameter of the alluvial material; K_s is the coefficient of total resistance, so that K_s/K_r expresses the reduction in mean speed which may be attributed to a cause other than the interaction of the water and the grains, in particular to the form of the bed. It varies between 1 when the bed is smooth, and 0.7 when dunes are well formed. I is the slope, H is the depth, and B a constant coefficient affected only by the specific gravity of the material.

A recent attempt has been made by Hans Albert Einstein, an American hydraulic engineer. This depends on the determination of fluctuations in the hydraulic lift as a function of the turbulence (an average variation of one-third by comparison with the median). The probability that a pebble of given size effects a displacement equal to the average free course can then be calculated. Thus a fairly complex formula has been derived expressing the capacity of transport in relation to the width of the bed. This is an insoluble integral which can only be represented by graphical methods (fig 6). Even the theoretical reasoning of Einstein is based on a certain number of empirical

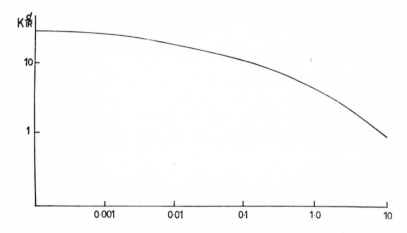

Fig 6   H. A. Einstein's curve showing the capacity of transport of a river per metre of width (transport of traction load). Logarithmic coordinates. The capacity of transport is shown on the abscissa

assumptions; for example, relating the average free movement to the diameter of the particle. Like the formula of Meyer-Peter, it shows the problem of establishing a fundamental distinction between the loss of energy by turbulence on the grains which alone would be responsible for moving the alluvial material, and that loss which results from irregularities of the bed. However, the eddies which are due to the bed irregularities may equally cause 'useful' movements.

As we have seen, none of the formulae expressing the capacity of transport can be applied to the derivation of the equation of the longitudinal profile of equilibrium, if one does not at the same time consider variations in the cross-profile of the bed. A fairly general

anology will show the factors that bear on this problem. Imagine
a trough down which roll a large number of ball bearings; there are
two ways of increasing the discharge: either the width of the trough
or the speed of movement of the balls may be increased. But the
speed at the base of the bed depends upon the hydraulic radius in a
rather complex way; it is proportional to the average speed which itself varies as $R^{⅔}$, but on the other hand, the relationship between the
average speed and the speed at the base of the bed is inversely proportional to the logarithm of R. Moreover, R becomes greater for a
given discharge as the depth/width ratio becomes greater (that is to
say, the width of the moving mass is relatively reduced). There is
consequently an optimum value of R, giving the greatest possible
value of the capacity of transport by a compromise between the increase of the width of the moving mass and the increase in the speed
at the bed. But this compromise must also take into account the competence which depends only on R.

Can this reasoning be made more quantitative on the basis of
formulae we have already established? In the first place all these
formulae include the product IR as an essential factor in the capacity
of transport per metre of width of the bed. Thus even in the limiting
case, where the increase of the wetted section downstream results only
from a linear increase of width (the average speed remaining constant), the hydraulic radius increases downstream, although the form of
this wetted section becomes more and more favourable. As a result the
solid discharge per metre of width of the bed can move over gentler
and gentler slopes, giving a concave longitudinal profile. But this is
true only of the limiting case; in actual fact the average speed is not
necessarily constant, the width increases more slowly than linearly,
and so on. When one attempts to calculate the optimum hydraulic
radius by applying Meyer-Peter's formula, it seems that in the upstream part of the course this optimum implies a wetted section that
is relatively deep in relation to the width, while downstream this relationship is reversed. The large number of measurements assembled
by Luna Leopold clearly show that in general, the width increases
more quickly than the depth as a function of the liquid discharge. A
stream may be three metres wide by one metre deep, a broad river
300 metres by five metres. This contrast follows from the fact that in
the upstream part, the total volume of traction load is small, but is
of large size; the factor of competence is more significant than
capacity. It is necessary to have the largest possible speed at the bed
of the stream, even if it is not very wide. As the load increases, it is

necessary to increase the width of the bed on which it moves, the movement of smaller, comminuted material being much easier. Finally, towards the mouth of the river, where a great proportion of the load is carried in suspension, the width of the bed can decrease again in agreement with the results assembled by Leopold. The cross-profile of equilibrium of the bed may well depend on other factors however; the irregularity of the discharge (which favours a relative increase in the width of the bed), the resistance of the river banks, and so on.

The discouraging result of these many attempts to calculate the capacity of transport is that we do not know the way this increases with discharge. A more fundamental line of research would be to discover experimentally to what extent the increase of discharge affects the crucial ratio between the energy dissipated in heat and that which is utilised for transport.

It has already been necessary to refer to the diameter of the alluvial material. It is a factor of very great importance which of itself may be used to justify the concavity of the river profile, as a function of the decrease in grain size downstream. In fact all the formulae which express the capacity of transport per metre of width, show that the capacity decreases more rapidly than linearly with d (maximum diameter of alluvial material). In the formula of Meyer-Peter, G_1 varies as $-d^{3/6}$ and in the curve by Einstein, while the decrease is almost linear for small values of d, it is much more rapid for larger values.

On what does this decrease in size of alluvial material depend? Firstly it is the result of wear at the bed itself. The further the alluvial material travels, the smaller in size it becomes. Two processes are involved here: one is the active wear of moving pebbles; they may bang against each other and shatter or may be worn away grain by grain by abrasion or chemical decomposition. In the first example there is an abrupt change, in the others the general form of the pebble is preserved. Secondly the pebbles also suffer passive wear; lying stationary on the bed they may be shattered or abraded by pebbles carried along by the stream. While the active wear is an exponential function of the distance x through which the alluvial material is moved, passive wear is a function of the time during which the material rests on the river bed. The formula adopted by Leopold and Maddock must be regarded as incomplete, as it uses only an exponential function of the distance from origin.

The other factor in the diminution of size of alluvial material is the decrease of the valleyside slopes downstream, because the size of material supplied to the stream depends essentially on the angle of slope. This can be demonstrated by the fact that where for some reason the load increases in calibre downstream, the longitudinal gradient of the river increases too. The Rhône below Lake Geneva, and the Saône, are rivers fed from areas of moderate relief. Then the Rhône is joined by the Isère; this drains part of the Alps and brings much larger material than that carried in the Rhône itself, and this immediately increases the gradient of the Rhône.

So far the discharge has been assumed to be constant, but major complications are introduced by seasonal fluctuations. On the one hand, the capacity of transport per metre of width of the bed increases more quickly than linearly with discharge; the result is that the total transporting capacity of a river becomes greater, the more the seasonal variation increases, other things being equal. On the other hand it is necessary to take into account the variation of the wetted section. The cross-profile of equilibrium, with its more or less clear distinction between flood-plain and the river channel, has been influenced by the frequency of different discharges, and cannot be understood without taking account of its histogram. Here it is impossible to proceed by quantitative *a priori* reasoning and it is therefore necessary to establish a theory on the basis of a number of particular cases. Leopold and Maddock have begun this task. One very simple case where there is no flood plain may be quoted. The increase of width as a function of discharge at the selected cross-section was to the power of o.3, the speed to the power of o.35. As the capacity of transport per metre of width is approximately proportional to V^3, the result is that this is a little more rapid than a linear increase (and an even more rapid increase for the total transport capacity if one takes into account the increase in width).

Outline of a practical programme for the study of the capacity of transport

In the present state of hydrodynamics, it is impossible to derive a precise formula expressing the transporting capacity of a river. It is not easy to separate quantitatively the relative influence of the increase in the discharge and of the decrease in size of the load on the shape of the profile, nor the different factors affecting this decrease in size. We must await the result of a systematic empirical comparison between the character of alluvial material and the long profile, using a similar approach to that of Leopold and Maddock. Here comment is restricted to suggesting a few ways in which research might be carried out.

The aim is to compare the long profile (on which the principal lithological boundaries are marked), the profile of liquid discharge, and the profile of solid discharge (including the grain size of the material). Such an investigation must not be limited to a point by point comparison of these hydraulic variables against the load. It must not be forgotten that the local erosive potential is immediately influenced by every variable of load upstream, and, after a greater or smaller delay, by every disturbance which affects the load downstream. These complications were not allowed for in the pioneering work of Iovanovic (1940).

It is relatively easy to determine the profile of liquid discharge. In the simplest cases, all that is needed is to measure the average discharge of the principal river and its major tributaries, and the departures from these mean values. It is possible to get an approximate idea of the law of increase in discharge downstream by calculating, for every point on the profile, the area of the drainage basin above that point. Where the basin is large, draining regions of contrasted run-off, gauge measurements are needed to draw a curve relating the discharge to distance from the source.

The curve of solid discharge can be established using the same principles in those very rare cases where engineers have built measuring facilities, constructions usually beyond the scope of geographers. In most cases one must be content with a study of the granulometry of the alluvial material at a number of points. The aim is to determine the law of diminution of the size of alluvial material for each rock type present as a function of the slope, the discharge, and the distance from the source.

Samples of alluvial material must be taken during periods when the water is sufficiently low to expose the higher parts of the river bed, or when the water depth enables easy sampling. In small streams, pebbles may be collected during periods of normal flow without making any distinction between the pools and shoals. A sample taken from the flood-plain will naturally have a completely different significance and is not comparable with other samples of alluvial material. If possible, it is desirable to choose a case where the flood-plain is well established so that samples from the river channel are uncontaminated by material from the slopes. If sites of this type cannot be found, the appearance of the slope detritus must be noted, for included with the truly fluvial material may be detritus derived directly from the valley slopes that has not been transported by water at all.

In areas where man has been active, there may be mill dams which retain the alluvial material. Downstream from the highest mill, the normal evolution of the alluvial material is restricted to separate sections between each mill. However, it is possible to draw some useful conclusions by examining the material retained behind each dam. If the alluvial material is mainly stony, one hundred pebbles may be collected at random (from an area about two metres square) starting with the largest pebble. Each pebble is weighed, to give the proportion by weight of each type of rock. The same operation is then repeated, this time taking the 100 largest pebbles of each rock type to determine the size and lithological composition of the coarsest part of the alluvium. Where the alluvial material includes a significant sand or clay fraction, it is necessary to take about one-tenth of a cubic metre and pass it through sieves to separate cobbles, gravel, sand and finer material. Each cobble is weighed as in the preceding observations, while the granulometric curve of the gravels can be established in the field by using sieves. One kilogramme of sand and the finer material is put into a sample bag for eventual granulometric analysis and for morphoscopic analysis of the sands.

If the river is large, samples should be taken from several different bars, for there are likely to be considerable variations in the proportion of pebbles to finer material. Thus it is eventually possible to establish the granulometry of all the alluvial material by weighing the various size fractions. Ideally one would drag the bed of the river to obtain a representative sample of the alluvial material.

Even where it is impossible to establish the curve of the solid discharge, one can draw useful conclusions by comparing the long profile of the curve of liquid discharge and the variations in the granulometry. First, it is important to distinguish the relative influence of the concentration of discharge and the decrease in size of the detritus on the concavity of the profile of equilibrium. If the confluence of an important tributary in an area of homogeneous rock expresses itself in a diminution of slope, this indicates that the capacity of transport increases very much more than the discharge. The angle at the change of slope is the quantitative measure of this phenomenon. A large number of such measurements will give a law of increase of capacity of transport as a function of the discharge. It is also desirable to take into consideration the granulometry of the load of each tributary.

If the confluence of a major tributary does not lead to a decrease of slope, and if the slope decreases progressively along the river where there are no important tributaries, this indicates that the decrease in size of the bed alluvium, as a function of distance, is the principal factor leading to the increase in the capacity of transport. This has been observed for a river in the u.s.a. (Mackin, 1948). An increase of slope downstream of a confluence can have a dual significance: (a) the tributary may bring a particularly large load exceeding the competence of the combined stream (as in the case already quoted of the Rhône below its confluence with the Isère); (b) alternatively the region may have been recently tilted so that the river finds itself in a state of disequilibrium. The increase in the capacity of transport of the main stream, resulting from a given increase in slope, is in general more than that which affects the tributaries. The penetration of the main river into a mountainous region where it receives a sequence of tributaries of increasingly steeper slope can lead to the development of a major convexity with progressive increase of slope downstream along the course of the main river. In all other cases, the existence of large convexities must often be interpreted as cases of hypothesis (b).

It is sometimes possible to distinguish the causes of the decrease in size of alluvial material, that is to say, between the effects of the reduction of valleyside slopes and wear of the bed load. This might be achieved by examining the granulometry of two reaches in the same rock separated by a reach of several tens of kilometres or more of another rock, the whole length in the same cycle of erosion. Four samples of the alluvium should be taken—in the case shown in fig 7, (1) some 15 km into the upstream granite, (2) at the upper granite-schist junction, (3) at the lower junction, and (4) after some 15 km through the lower granite. The granulometric curve corresponding to sample (4) will carry a double maximum because the pebbles of granite will have been derived from either the upstream or downstream outcrop. The comparison of the size curve for station (1) with the portion of the curve for station (4) corresponding to the incoming of the downstream granite, allows the isolation of the influence of the widening of the valley downstream; taken as a whole the detritus must be smaller. The decrease in size shown by a comparison between curves (2) and (3) will demonstrate the result of bed wear alone.

The decrease in size between sites (2) and (3) could be the result either of progressive wear or sorting. These may be distinguished by analysing the proportion of unresistant rocks in the alluvial material.

Let us suppose that upstream equal surfaces with a steep slope provide equal amounts of resistant and unresistant material of the same size. If the phenomenon of sorting is dominant, the proportion of fragile elements will increase downstream. This is because these are worn more quickly and their reduced size enables them to be transported further, while the resistant pebbles retain their size and are left, by sorting, upstream. A similar criterion is a sharp decrease of size, particularly of resistant pebbles. If wear is the main cause for the

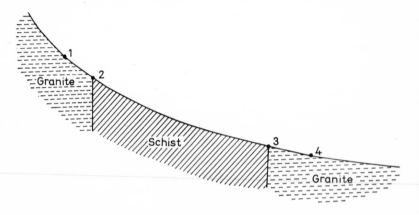

Fig 7   Longitudinal profile of a valley crossing a schistose slope between two granite masses. The figures indicate the sampling points for the alluvial material

decrease in size of alluvial material, this will give an increase in the relative proportion of resistant material along the river.

When sorting is the predominant cause of the reduction in size, with a consequent accumulation of the larger material upstream, the régime is, by definition, not an equilibrium régime but one of deposition (*régime de remblaiement*). In practice the recognition of equilibrium in rivers is very difficult. Some indication is provided by the shape of the long profile as it crosses a band of hard rock between two broad outcrops of weaker rock. If the river increases in gradient as it crosses the hard rock, three interpretations are possible:

(a) The provisional profile of equilibrium has not yet been reached and the river is at present actively downcutting (*régime de creusement*).

(b) The river is in a state of equilibrium, but the valleysides in the hard rock provide large material which exceeds the competence of the river, necessitating an increase in the gradient of the river to achieve its removal. Naturally the larger the area of hard rock, the more likely is this state of affairs.

(c) The constriction of the bed in the hard rock by the limitation of lateral erosion can force the river to increase its gradient, to offset the decrease in bed width, which would otherwise reduce its ability to transport.

Conversely, the absence of a break of slope where the river crosses a band of hard rock is clear evidence that a profile of equilibrium has been attained (or has even been passed if deposition is occurring everywhere). It may be noted that those bands of rock which are so resistant that they are totally immune to decomposition (or decay immediately to fine material) will not cause breaks in the profile of equilibrium.

The distinction between cases (a), (b) and (c), is not always easy. Certainly the presence of a continuous layer of alluvial material at the base of the bed indicates that the provisional profile of equilibrium has been reached. But there may be doubtful situations where the base may be formed of blocks of the hard rock the river is crossing. These can equally well be interpreted either as rocks which have been incompletely removed from the bed in a régime of incision which has not yet reached equilibrium (case a), or as large material from the slopes on the hard rock forcing the river to increase its gradient although remaining in equilibrium (case b). The presence of an entirely rocky bed suggests that the river is still actively downcutting and has yet to reach equilibrium; a likely suggestion as the increase of gradient has evidently not been made necessary by the difficulty of removing large blocks exceeding the competence of the river. This will be equally true for the case where the river channel is rocky and the flood plain has an alluvial cover, since this flood plain separates the slopes from the river bed. However, a few steep tributaries could carry the blocks to the main river.

The most usual arrangement in areas of sufficiently strong relief is the presence of a break of slope with a rocky channel where it crosses a hard band, whereas both above and below this section, the profile is less steep and the cover of alluvial material on the bed is continuous. It must be concluded that a recent change decreasing the discharge load ratio has caused deposition in the less steep sectors of a long profile which had not reached its provisional profile of equilibrium during a previous climatic phase. Within the hard rock, the gradient is sufficient to enable the complete removal of the material brought from upstream. One can also envisage partial profiles of equilibrium developed solely on sections of weak rock, where incision is no longer a function of the decrease in size of the load provided by the slopes. The break of slope on the hard rocks, in this case, represents a residual phenomenon which may disappear only very slowly.

The essential object of this study remains the determination of the relationship between the major characteristics of the slopes of a river basin and its loss of material, and this can only be achieved in the very rare cases where the traction load is known. The study of a number of reservoir catchments in the western u.s.a. has suggested that there is an exponential relationship between the tonnage of material collected in the reservoir and the 'relief ratio', i.e. the relationship between the maximum amount of relief of a basin and its major axis. The loss of material would increase much more rapidly than linearly with the average slope. But it seems necessary to include the absolute value of the length of this long axis, so following the ideas of J. Blanche.

The erosion of rock in situ

When the transporting capacity and the competence of a river exceed the load provided by the slopes, there is an erosive potential proportional to this excess, and vertical incision begins. So long as the material eroded is alluvium or soft rock, the processes of excavation are analogous to those which are responsible for transport. This is a rapid process; the construction of the Hoover Dam, which deprived the Colorado of its load, gave an erosive potential which enabled the river to incise itself three metres in a few years without any increase in gradient.

Erosion of resistant rock sets in motion processes of a different type which are still imperfectly understood, although this is a fundamental aspect of geomorphology. These processes take place much more slowly, and certain authors such as J. Bourcart consider that fluvial erosion is, in general, incapable of attacking in any real sense a coherent resistant rock. According to him, apart from exceptional cases, fluvial erosion can only exploit lines of weakness (joints in the granite, tension fissures along anticlines in limestones, etc.) or layers which have been partially decomposed by weathering below the stream bed. An example of this is provided by P. Fénelon, according to whom the Charente does not at present attack the limestone slopes but is merely removing the products of frost action.

It appears difficult to maintain such an extreme position. The mere existence of incised meanders with rocky cliffs shows clearly that a river is capable of eroding such rocks into a form absolutely independent of any structural control and which only depends on hydrological factors (the discharge, slope, and so on). Naturally, in each case, careful examination is necessary to determine to what extent the river has cut into rock which is already decomposed, accelerating this physical-chemical decomposition, or to what extent it has mechanically attacked fresh rock. The occurrence of overhangs provides decisive proof of such incision in fresh rock.

It is in the beds of streams with waterfalls that the most obvious proof of fluvial mechanical action may be found. Eddies with horizontal axes and armed with pebbles cut hollows in the bed and score the intervening sills. But it is the whirlpools with vertical axes which cut giant potholes. These phenomena are not only found in the beds of sub-glacial streams as has been proposed for the Valserine; they are met in all climates, for example the torrents of the Itatiaia massif in Brazil. The accelerated erosion found below waterfalls is largely a result of the coalescence of these potholes. Moreover, on the face of the fall, the projections are reduced as a result of repeated shattering. Upstream of the falls, the speeding up of the water leads to erosion by striation if the river is carrying pebbles, which is not always the case. By contrast, pebbles are always found at the base of the waterfall since they are derived from the face. The direct action of the fall of water itself varies greatly with the volume and height of the fall. The impact of a waterfall of small discharge but great height has little mechanical effect, since the water breaks up into a cloud of spray. A low fall of large volume is much more effective.

One suspects that an important factor in this torrential erosion is the phenomenon of 'cavitation', known from the damage suffered by man-made steel conduits. Rapid and irregular flow of water forms pockets where the pressure decreases sharply so that the water partially vaporises (at the same time liberating dissolved air). A sharp disturbance breaks up these pockets and in filling them the water sharply attacks the sides. But this phenomenon can only be produced in very steep torrents, which at the same time do not lose contact with the surface over which they flow; a minimum speed of 13 metres per second must be reached. In theory, this phenomenon is effective even where the stream carries no rock fragments.

A vital task is the evaluation of the speed of these erosional processes. The great fall at Niagara, which is cutting at its base into relatively unresistant shales, has receded by 60 cm per year. Where traces of old potholes are found several metres above a stream, without the rock showing any signs of physical-chemical decomposition, one can at least deduce that vertical erosion works at a speed incomparably greater than the evolution of the slopes (though it must not be forgotten that as the rock is polished it will break up less readily).

PART TWO

The influence of different climates on the cycle of erosion

Introduction

The effect of different climates on the progress of the cycle of erosion is accomplished, either directly or indirectly, through the factor of vegetation. The direct effect is chiefly significant for its control over the relative importance of different factors of rock decomposition and of agents of transport on slopes. In most climates all types of weathering exist together, just as all types of transport will be found on the same slope. But their relative importance varies. On the other hand there are some processes, such as the action of ice, which are limited to certain climatic zones. Climate also has a direct effect on linear erosion. This will vary with the average discharge per square metre of surface which is a function of the annual precipitation/evaporation balance. It is also important to consider seasonal or annual variations. One river may have the same average discharge as another, but if one has a great variation in flow between low water and floods, it will have a much greater capacity of transport. More significant still is the indirect action of climate, through the intermediary of vegetation, and as a result vegetation will be used as the basis of the classification of systems of erosion. Firstly the vegetation is an important agent in the process of rock decomposition (whether living, i.e. through the roots, or dead) and secondly it controls the conditions under which detritus is carried on the slopes.

In those cases where the soil is covered by a continuous plant cover, all the agents of transport are obstructed, particularly wash. In forest, even if the ground flora is not completely continuous, the fallen leaves give a thick litter that absorbs rain water. If this layer becomes saturated, surface wash is almost entirely involved in removing the organic material. By contrast, if the vegetation is discontinuous, all transport processes can occur, including wind erosion. This is the fundamental distinction in climatic geomorphology.

Within the zone with a continuous plant cover, it is necessary to distinguish between temperate forest and tropical rain forest. In temperate forests all weathering processes occur, including frost action, as do all methods of transport, so that this has some claim to be recognised as the normal model of the systems of erosion. By contrast the tropical rain forest is characterised by the absence of frost action and the preponderance of chemical decomposition. A continuous vegetation cover is also found in the grasslands, but the study of these has only just begun (Tricart 1953). Further, most areas of grassland in the world coincide with plains, that is to say, with areas where it is not possible to study the complete cycle of erosion. This is not accidental for almost always the grassland is due not merely to climatic control, but also due to a textural factor as has been shown by Walther: the predominance of fine materials. As soon as coarser material outcrops woody vegetation occurs, clinging to joints. And so this brings us again to the case of discontinuous plant cover.[1]

This second major group, a discontinuous vegetation cover, shows two principal sub-divisions; the hot semi-arid areas (or at least those with a long dry season), and the periglacial areas. Here it is important to note that a cycle of erosion that attacks an area of appreciable relief (e.g. a mountain some 2,000 metres high) develops in different climatic conditions simply as a result of the range of altitude involved. For a cycle of erosion in the temperate zone, the role of frost action is important in all the higher areas.

To establish the basis of a climatic geomorphology would seem to be easy: study the forms and the processes in selected parts of each climatic zone and, from this, deduce the evolution of the cycle of erosion. Unfortunately this method, although apparently the most logical and simple, cannot be used. The reason is that in almost all areas of the world the frequency of climatic change has meant that hardly anywhere has an area developed under a single climate throughout the whole of an erosion cycle. This is certainly the impression gained from a study of the Quaternary period. Is this an illusion: has the appearance of man coincided with a particularly disturbed stage in the development of the planet? Even in the tropical world which has been regarded as stable, even on relatively steep slopes, it seems necessary to have recourse to climatic changes, to

[1] This fundamental distinction approximately corresponds to that proposed by Tricart. But the terms selected by him—climates with chemical erosion and with mechanical erosion—have the disadvantage that they allow the continuation of the error that in dry climates disintegration is of a purely thermal origin (which does not seem to be what the author intended).

palaeoclimates, to understand the details of the erosion, the peculiarities of the soil and alluvial material. The erosional zones to which we are accustomed are the result of the integration of very different sequences of successive erosional systems.

Moving from the Pole towards the Equator, there is first an *Arctic zone* which includes interior Alaska, Northern Siberia, etc. In the simplest cases, which were dry and so unglaciated in the Pleistocene, a temperate Tertiary climate was followed by a periglacial climate during the Pleistocene. In similarly unglaciated areas in the *Temperate zone* the succession has been: an early Tertiary tropical climate, subtropical in the Mio-Pliocene and then during the Quaternary, phases of periglacial climate alternated with sub-tropical or temperate climates of the Mediterranean or Chinese type. The *Intertropical zone* has not experienced a periglacial climate, but it is impossible to find a region which has not experienced both hot–dry and hot–wet climates. Aeolian sands cover southern Africa as far as the Equator, while ferruginous crusts and aeolian pebbles extend south to the coast in West Africa. This leaves little room for any permanent humid equatorial zone. Conversely, even in the heart of the Sahara, recent investigations have shown the existence of lateritic clays of Tertiary age. All that can be said is that in one region or another dry or wet periods have been predominant during that part of geological time which has seen the formation of the present landscape. It must not be forgotten that the morphological significance of any system of erosion is not simply a function of its duration. Long, arid periods are perhaps restricted to preserving a relief evolved in much shorter, humid periods. It may even be necessary to go further and to suggest that effective erosion is characteristic not of an equilibrium state with a constant climate, but specifically of crises provoked by a succession of different climates.

It is impossible to erect a simple scheme based on observed facts; we are forced to construct a theoretical climatic geomorphology by trying to visualise what would happen if the climate were always wet, or always dry. This must naturally be based on the evidence we have of the actual progress of erosion in the few thousand years that have followed the last climatic revolution, during the last glacial period, the last 'pluvial' period, and also in laboratory experiments. The examination of palaeosols (the evidence of past climates), or of polygenetic soils which include characteristics acquired in successive climates, show that slopes have undergone relatively little denudation since this last climatic change. These polygenetic soils may survive even on relatively steep slopes of perhaps as much as 20°. Naturally the more the present climate favours erosion, the stronger the chance of making a correct evaluation of the effects of contemporary processes. In this respect tropical–humid and periglacial–humid climates are the most suitable.

4 The evolution of the cycle under a normal climate

It is helpful to consider first the evolution of the cycle of erosion under a 'normal' climate such as is found in temperate and sub-tropical zones that have a forest cover. This choice is not inspired by a sentimental attachment to Davisian tradition. The climatic zones considered are characterised by an extreme variety of methods of rock decomposition (from ice-action to very rapid clay formation in the brown forest soils) as well as in the methods of transportation on the slopes: all types are represented without any one of them becoming particularly predominant. One problem, however, is that the influence of palaeoclimates, even on relatively steep slopes, is more complex than elsewhere. Even on slopes as steep as $15°-20°$, where present erosion cannot be negligible, characteristic indications of congeliturbation indicate that much of the soil dates from the last periglacial phase. Large boulders found within finer material are generally attributed to this past period rather than to the action of frost today. Finally, recent climatic accidents have probably led to abnormal variations in the thickness of colluvial material accumulated at the foot of the slopes. The objective separation of the true 'normal' cycle of erosion is thus made very difficult.

We will take the most general (or at any rate most complete) case where the cycle of erosion passes through a youthful phase. We will then examine the result of rejuvenation of the slopes (for example following a tilting movement), and on the other hand the attack of erosion on tectonic slopes created by abrupt movements.

Tilting movements affecting a block which has reached old age are likely to include a short phase during which there is an increasing speed of earth movement, followed by a stage of decreasing movement. During the first phase the streams incise themselves at an increased rate which quickly exceeds the speed of denudation of the

slopes. Thus the slopes steepen by developing a convexity. This increase of slope speeds up the rate of movement of the material on the
slopes. The regolith which was slipping slowly under the effects of
creep and flow is first stripped close to the talweg where the slope is
at a maximum. The increased flow (sometimes assisted by landslips)
proceeds more quickly than rock decomposition so that fresh rock
outcrops. At the same time the plant cover deteriorates. Wash then
clears off the fine material and henceforward on the denuded valley
side the loss of material proceeds under the direct influence of gravity
carrying along the larger blocks towards the base. In the normal
climate envisaged, this process occurs when a slope reaches about
40° as can be seen in the youthful valleys of the Palaeozoic uplands.

What is the further evolution of this rocky slope? It seems that it
must retreat parallel to itself, for there is no reason why the loss of
material should be more significant in one part than another. Blocks
detached from the slope slide along the joints, which are less steep
than the valley slope, but are steeper than the angle at which friction
would no longer allow them to move. This process begins in the upper
part of the slope and spreads towards the bottom as fast as each block
is freed from that above. In principle, this propagation must be very
rapid and it does not at any time influence the form of the slope, given
always that the coefficient of friction is the same throughout the
whole of the slope. This coefficient depends principally on moisture.
The separation of the blocks is aided by the presence either of a thin
layer of ice along the joints or of plant roots, or of a clay layer which
acts as a lubricant. Although the lower part of the slope is crossed by
all the water which falls on the slope above, on the other hand because the slope is convex, this water is moving more quickly. There
does not seem to be any reason why the loss of material should vary
systematically over the slope, as a whole, so long as it is not influenced
by what is happening in the neighbourhood of the local base-level.
From this it appears that there should be a re-examination of the
hypothesis put forward by J. Bakker, according to whom the bare
slope will pivot and decline in a systematic manner (*central linear
recession*).

It must be noted that the evolution of a bare slope follows very
different laws from those applying to covered slopes. The wider apart
the joints are, the larger the blocks and the more chance they have of
moving, without stopping, to the foot of the slope. In the course of
their movement they acquire a considerable momentum which
enables them to cross narrow flats or even short areas of reversed

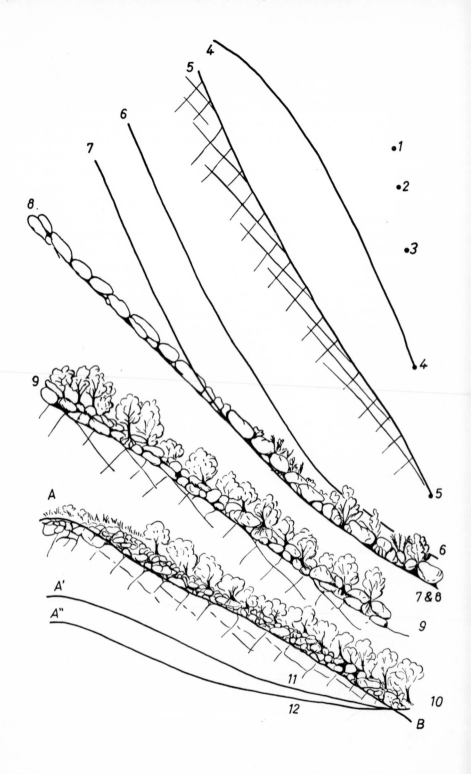

slope which will hold material of smaller calibre for a long time. By contrast it is known that on all other types of slope the movement of detritus is inversely proportional to the size of the particles. As the loss of material by slips becomes more rapid as the slope gets steeper, the lower part of the convexity retreats at the expense of the upper part: thus is formed a rectilinear slope of great uniformity (*Steilrelief* of W. Penck). But the extent to which the slopes retreat depends mainly on the density of the drainage network and the ability of the tributaries to keep pace with the incision of the main stream.

This incision of the main river will slow down for a variety of reasons. First of all the tilting itself reaches a phase of deceleration. Then the slope of the stream decreases automatically in the course of its incision, for the level of the mouth is fixed. Finally the quantity of detritus provided by the slopes increases in proportion to their lengthening and the increase in their average slope. There then comes a time when the erosive potential of the stream will only permit, in a given unit of time, a vertical incision which is less than the maximum thickness of material lost by the slopes. In the neighbourhood of the talweg a zone of concave slopes now begins to replace the rectilinear steep slope. On this declining slope, the large blocks will not be able to move as easily, while on the other hand there will inevitably come

Fig 8 Evolution of a slope during the course of a complete cycle of erosion in a normal climate (temperate moist climate). From 1 to 5, phases of accelerated erosion. The points indicate the positions of the talweg. In 5 is indicated the network of joints in the solid rock. The inclination of the joints in relation to the valley side is assumed to be greater than the angle of equilibrium of the blocks. From 5 to 8, phases of retarded incision up to the establishment of a provisional profile of equilibrium of the talweg. The decrease in angle of the lower part of the slope which formed as a result of the retreat of the upper part parallel to itself places a limit on the slipping of blocks by simple gravity. These accumulate first of all at the base, in 8, then extend to occupy the whole slope. In 9 vegetation has colonised the whole of the slope. The production of fine material is active both at the surface and within the joints. In 10 the upper portion becomes mobile and slips in a manner conforming to the laws of plastic bodies. Thus the soil thickness is reduced at A, and the slope decomposes rapidly, leading in the upper part to the creation of a convex slope. In 11 the transverse profile of equilibrium with convexity above and concavity below. In 12 the state of the slope in a stage close to senility

a time when the river will only just be able to remove the rocks provided by the slopes. This is an essential phase in the evolution, the
transition to a *régime of provisional equilibrium*, where the incision of the
talweg is no longer determined, even indirectly, by tectonic forces,
but by the processes of slope development.

At the same time these slopes undergo a profound change: the
appearance of a cover of detritus. In fact, from the moment when the
action of the river is limited to the transport of detritus, the bed is
provisionally stabilised, while the slope continues to retreat. But the
lower part of the valley side must remain steep enough to allow the
removal of the large blocks as they are produced; these are 'Richter
slopes' in Bakker's terminology. They are of the order of magnitude
of 30°–38° and must be the steeper where the blocks have less momentum as the result of a shorter fall. In principle these Richter slopes
must extend by regressive erosion across all the slope, becoming
steeper towards the top. But in the humid zone now being considered,
this evolution is interrupted by the action of vegetation. This becomes well-established in joints on slopes of less than 40°. On the
upper part of the slope trees contribute to the loosening of blocks, but
lower down their trunks obstruct falling blocks. These will now only
move when the tree dies, a form of progress related to creep. By
regressive accumulation, the whole slope tends to be covered by
blocks. The talus is stabilised, allowing time for physical-chemical
processes to produce a much greater quantity of smaller detritus.
Part of this finer material will still be moved by wash, but the vegetation will retain the rest, while in its turn, the presence of this fine
material assists the establishment of a herbaceous cover. Thus there
inevitably develops a covered slope where the removal of detritus
takes place slowly, and the more efficiently as the detritus becomes
finer. In particular, flow can only occur when a fine matrix becomes
available that will carry the blocks along, while the size of the blocks
must be sufficiently reduced to allow them to move between the roots
of the trees.

The soil thus behaves approximately as a plastic body, the bending
of tree trunks showing the deformation down the slope. In the whole
deformed mass the component of shearing, which is generally parallel
to the slope, exceeds the threshold of plasticity:

$$h \sin \alpha > h \cos \alpha \tan \rho_0 + c$$

h being the distance of the point from the surface and $\tan \rho_0$ being
the angle of internal friction, c being the cohesion (see fig 9).

Because of the effect of the factor h, deformation only begins at a certain depth. The water content, which decreases tan ρ_0 and c, is also less variable from one season to another at depth. In the case of a perched water table, the hydrostatic pressure decreases towards the surface in the same way as atmospheric pressure decreases with altitude. A compensating factor must be noted however: the increase of compaction under the weight of overlying ground which increases tan ρ_0.

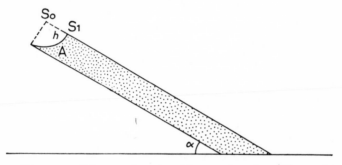

Fig 9   Deep regolith on a slope is subject to shearing. (For explanation of letters see text)

Henceforth the evolution of the slopes depends on a complex equilibrium between two closely interdependent factors: the decomposition of rock *in situ* and the removal of detritus downhill. These two processes operate at about the same speed (on a bare slope the speed of removal is almost infinite compared with the speed of decomposition). The speed of disintegration depends on the thickness of the detritus. On the one hand it is essential that this material should be capable of holding water for as long as possible, but on the other hand thermal variations decrease with depth. We have seen that these thermal variations play an important role, both in leading to freeze-thaw action and in making the rock permeable. Finally, as chemical decomposition increases exponentially with temperature (its speed doubles with an increase in temperature of 10°C.), it is much more rapid in the upper layers where the temperature reaches high maxima than in the lower horizons where the temperature is relatively constant. This is relevant even for the solution of limestone, at least under certain climates, for although the amount of carbon dioxide in solution (to form carbonic acid) decreases as the temperature increases, the speed of the reaction follows the general law. It must be added, that beyond a certain depth (about one metre), the action of both living and dead vegetation decreases considerably, for at this depth there are only a few, isolated, large roots. Finally the weight of the soil hinders the breaking up of the fresh rock by the expansion of salts, colloids or clays. The interaction of these complex factors, often working with opposed effects, gives an optimum thickness of detritus; in the temperate climate we are considering this will be of the order of 30 cm; where the detritus is thinner, inadequate retention of water is a limiting factor; with thicker detritus the controls are the small thermal variations and the reduction in the number of roots. This optimum thickness is also the virtual limit of frost action in temperate oceanic areas.

The thickness of the detritus itself depends on the speed of removal, and is inversely proportional to it where flow is the dominant agent. This speed of removal is approximately proportional to αh, α being the angle of slope and h the thickness. It is possible to apply the law of deformation of plastic bodies; in these conditions of laminar flow, the speed decreases linearly downwards, and one may compare the section of colluvial soil to a parallelogram which is deformed with time. However, the uppermost part of the detritus is also affected by creep with a speed of displacement proportional to the angle of slope α. In a temperate climate it is probable that creep considerably increases the speed of movement of this uppermost layer. The angle of slope is also important in determining the depth to which the regolith is mobile, i.e. the depth of the colluvial layer. In general rock fragments in the soil increase in size with depth and so the minimum angle necessary for their movement becomes greater. But the depth of this limiting layer depends also on the thickness of the mobile detritus above it; that is to say, on all the other factors which control the degree of mobility of the soil. The most important of these are the soil texture, the clay type and the water content. This water content is itself inversely proportional to the slope, and becomes greater downslope where the percolating water is increased by groundwater moving from upslope. In addition, the finer the texture, the more water is retained, even during drought. The surface movement due to wash is closely dependent on the permeability of the soil. In the upper part of the slope, ground water (a factor in flow) and surface water (a factor in wash) vary inversely to each other. But in the lower part of the slope, saturation of all the pore spaces will occur at least at certain periods of the year, making surface wash possible.

The angle of slope is itself directly determined by the speed of production of movable detritus at two consecutive points on the slope. This brief, and still incomplete, analysis of the interrelations of the different factors which affect the evolution of a slope, gives an idea of the difficulty of quantitative study and the derivation of an equation. The latter must be preceded by a large number of analyses of sample slopes, using the statistical and dynamic methods we have already described. One of the essential tasks of statistical analysis is to determine: (1) for each vertical section, the increase in size of detritus down to the lower limit of the mobile layers; and (2) by sampling at constant depths, the rate in decrease of size downslope. The latter is the result of both the speed of movement and the speed of wear as a function of time. Meanwhile, certain qualitative hypotheses can be suggested, accounting for the development of a mature slope with a convex upper sector and concave below, and with an approximately constant thickness of detritus.

It is possible to understand fairly readily the development of the upper convexity, even from the intersection of straight slopes. So long as the soil is thin, the convergence of subaerial weathering (infiltrating water and temperature variations in particular) tends to transform the sharp angle into a convexity. This convexity automatically tends to extend downwards because convergence similarly affects the junction of the convex slope and the slope below which preserves its original steepness. The angle of this lower slope may even increase, if we concede that at this stage the speed of decomposition of the rock is proportional to the thickness of the soil layer. Soil depth will tend to increase along a rectilinear slope, for the speed of disintegration and the speed of transport are of the same order of magnitude. Thus a very marked convexity tends to develop on the upper part of the slope.

The convexity changes when the law of decomposition of rock reverses, that is when it becomes inversely proportional to the thickness of detritus. At the top of the ridge, the debris tends to thin out as it moves. Decomposition of the downslope part takes place only very slowly whereas that of the upper part is increased. This phenomenon will continue up to the time when the increase in slope of the lower part gives an increase in speed to the detritus that exactly compensates the arrival of new material provided per unit area. Thus the increased discharge does not lead to an increase in soil depth. From the time when this depth becomes constant, the supply of material becomes equally uniform over the whole of the convex slope which from then on evolves parallel to itself. It is also necessary to take into account the increase in mobility that results from the decomposition of detritus in the course of its movement.

It must not be forgotten that the soil is deformed in a solid manner. On a convex slope, if the lower part begins to move more rapidly, it will exert a tensional stress on the slope above which will lead to movement.

The explanation of the concavity at the foot of the slope presents several major difficulties. Undoubtedly the cessation of active incision by the stream as a result of the establishment of a régime of provisional equilibrium, and the fact that in any case vertical incision remains less than the loss of material from the slopes, eventually leads to the development of a concave section. But it is necessary to explain why the thickness of detritus remains constant, despite the decrease in the slope. H. Baulig has explained this fact by suggesting that wash becomes the major transporting agent at the base of the slope because the detritus decays as it moves, and because the very fine texture makes the soil almost completely impermeable. This impermeability would also result from the downslope increase in soil water. The transporting action of wash may be likened to that of a stream, which as we know has a concave profile of equilibrium.

Several objections have been made to this seductive theory. Certainly in the case of a spring the increase in the amount of ground water downslope causes a sharp inflection. But the latter flows away along a channel. It is not a priori certain that the laws that control the profile of equilibrium of sheet flood or of anastomosed rills are the same as those of a well-defined channel; we have already seen how complex must be the justification of the concavity of the latter. Finally, although there are no precise measurements, one may disagree with the suggestion that wash is the major agent of transport under temperate forest, even at the foot of a slope.

The negative conclusions of A. Cailleux were based on sandy slopes of the Forêt de Rambouillet. They should not be generalised a priori and applied to less permeable rocks. It seems that at the end of winter on icy or saturated slopes, the role of surface flow may be significant. It can be enough to carry silts or very fine sands provided that the mineral soil is exposed; where this is obscured by an organic layer it will appear here and there through the actions of rodents or falling trees (at any rate in virgin forest). Moreover, the tendency towards flow varies widely with soil type, which shows great variations in the temperate zone. Flow reaches its maximum value in the soils of low mountains which are relatively warm and wet, where

silica and hydroxides are in large part peptised; its lowest values
occur in soils with aggregates, with chernozems as an extreme case.
In the absence of quantitative evidence, it would seem desirable to
preserve the most general explanation, in which the simultaneous
increase in the fineness of material and of its retention of water
increases the efficiency of all the agents of transport to the
point of enabling them to remove material on gentler and gentler
slopes.

These considerations explain how the concavity climbs higher as
the slope lengthens, for in the course of its movement, the detritus has
time to decrease in size and the liquid discharge has reached a value
which is adequate to saturate soils of a given thickness. Similarly one
may understand why convex slopes may descend further down on
spurs than on re-entrants because the proportion of far-travelled
debris derived from the top of the slope is greater in the second case
than the first (Birot, 1949, p. 37) and because there is a divergence
of the water movement in the first case and a convergence in the
second.

In regard to the upper convexity, we may invoke the solidity of the
soil cover. The lower part with the gentler slope is subject to pressure
from the steeper, upper part (compressional flow), and this force is
proportional to the length of the slope below the point of inflection.
The detritus can then move across a more gentle slope than would
otherwise be required. It is only on either side of the point of inflection that the slope is affected by local factors alone without these
complications of compression and tension. Thus the point of inflection
exists as a straight line of varying length.

How does evolution of the slope continue towards old age? The
essential fact is that the upper convex part of the slope declines more
quickly than the talweg, so the average slope decreases, the movement of detritus becomes slower while the thickness of soil increases
and the comminution of grain size of debris as a function of distance
from the top of the slope becomes more and more appreciable. This
leads to an increase in the concave part of the slope. Nevertheless an
opposing factor must not be forgotten, the increase in the thickness
of the soil and fineness of the detritus enables them to have greater
mobility, but this factor remains subordinate to the consequences of
the decline in slope. Moreover the evolution of the slope becomes
progressively slower. The decrease of speed of movement immediately
affects the speed of mass wasting which is also hindered by the increased soil thickness (giving a slower rate of decomposition of the

rock). Wear at the summit itself becomes progressively slower for this reason.

Thus this evolution involves essentially the decline of the whole slope, the curvature of the concavity remaining always very gentle. This last feature is a characteristic of temperate climates. In these conditions, in fact, every steep slope provides large detritus which decomposes slowly as it moves across the slope, and which can only be removed by such processes as flow. The detritus moves across a slope, each succeeding part of which is only slightly more gentle than the section above. A gentle equilibrium slope can then only be developed at the base if it is sufficiently far from sections with a steep slope. Such are the outstanding consequences of the relative slowness of chemical decomposition and the predominance of creep or flow as agents of transport. Thus the cycle evolves towards the peneplain.

The reconstruction of what happens in the phase of youth is much more difficult when the cycle of erosion is initiated by tectonic movements creating an entirely new relief, and where, consequently, the vocabulary of the cycle ceases to be exact. Apart from very exceptional cases (a very arid climate or very sudden tectonic movement) the forms which appear may be termed 'pene-primitive' and are the result of erosion proceeding at the same time as the movement. In general, this is limited to forming faceted faults and quasi-structural surfaces on the sides of anticlinal mountains. In both cases, the slopes are derived from regular surfaces, or even from perfect planes (fault planes), and preserve this character as long as valleys do not develop at right angles to the dislocation. Once they are formed, all the rock slopes evolve at a comparable speed, so that the existence of these pene-primitive forms is limited to the time necessary for the incision of the orthogonal talwegs.

The most frequently studied example is the evolution of fault escarpments. Normal faults have an average dip of 60°, a value which exceeds that of the majority of known facets. These facets must, then, result from erosion contemporaneous with the dislocation but which has not changed the original plane form. The problem is to understand why an initial rock slope is worn more quickly in its upper part. We have seen that at least in a sufficiently humid climate a 'central linear recession' would hardly be likely. But if we admit that the wear is contemporaneous with the uplift, we can realise that the upper part would undergo a larger loss of material from the plane of the original fault.

At the foot of the facets, the counterpart of this weathering is

represented by the accumulation of talus material. This slowly obscures the rock face, fossilising a convex slope: indeed as the rock face
decreases in area (by the simple fact that the material obscures it),
it provides a decreasing quantity of detritus per unit time. The
gradual rise of the talus up the face is slowed down in comparison

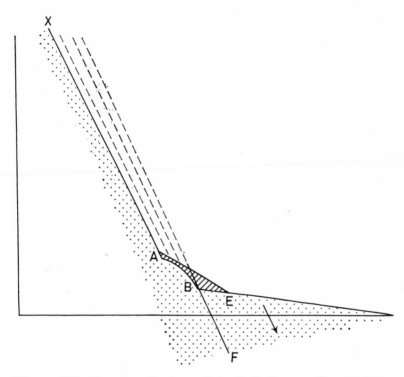

Fig 10   The first stages in the erosion of a fault scarp. On the right
the downthrow side. A large part of the talus has not been removed
and forms scree (obliquely shaded), while the face of the upthrow
side moves back as far as AX. AB is the buried profile, the curve of
which can be calculated accurately

with retreat of the upper rocky part. The curve of this fossilised slope
can be precisely established, as has been shown by Lehmann in a
differential equation which has been further improved by Bakker.
This is one of the few major successes of mathematical geomorphology.
But it should be noted that this evolution of talus slopes cannot be
generalised; it applies only to the case where there has been a sudden

disturbance of equilibrium, a tectonic movement (which is the case we have considered), and then only on the outward margins of the upraised mass. Another case is when a climatic disturbance replaces one system of erosion by another (for example glacial erosion instead of normal erosion). It is, then, scarcely likely that the convex slopes of our uplands could result from their exhumation by the removal of ancient material, as suggested by Bakker.

A still more straightforward case is that of a cliff abandoned by the sea. One generally observes that the fragments of Richter slopes which tend to develop are followed downslope by concave talus. Here again the presence of vegetation allows the formation of a mixture of blocks and fine material so that the debris can move on a more gentle slope (see the precise measurements made by Savigear, 1952).

5 The cycle of erosion in a tropical climate

The characteristics which distinguish the tropical cycle

A comparison with the system of erosion under temperate forest will show the essential features in the evolution of the cycle of erosion in a tropical humid climate. It can be put in the form of a double contrast: compared with temperate climates, *the decomposition of the rock* (mainly the result of chemical weathering) *is more rapid than the transport of material on the slopes*, which in turn *is more effective than fluvial erosion.*

The first of these contrasts impresses the most casual observer and is manifest in the enormous depth of soils (*sensu lato*). While in temperate regions, soil depths do not exceed two metres (and are often between 30 and 40 cm on slopes of 30°), the crystalline massifs of the Rio de Janeiro region, for example, are sometimes decomposed to a depth of 80 to 100 metres. The slopes of convex summits called 'half oranges' show soils 15 to 20 cm deep on slopes of 30° to 36°. In mountainous areas one finds soils of as much as 30 to 40 cm even on slopes as steep as 60°. Thus it is possible to use a bulldozer to lay out straight roads across gneissic spurs, or to level complete hills to construct a new suburb.

Such cuts show that only a small proportion of this friable layer is in movement. The normal profile which is found throughout humid Brazil poses very delicate problems if it is to be fully understood. It consists of an upper horizon of a yellow colour, below that a red horizon, and finally a pale, mottled horizon that gradually passes into fresh rock. Wherever quartz fragments are available from veins or derived pebbles they occur at the base of the upper, yellow horizon and are carried along by creep and flow, so that they form a regular layer over all the slope (stone-line). Sometimes they are also mixed with yellow earth. In the lower, red horizon (which is rich in clay), and in the white and mottled horizon, the quartz veins have preserved their original position; the only displacement of mineral material is by solution. Thus only the yellow horizon is mobile, and its thickness varies from a few tens of centimetres to three or four metres. On the moderate slopes of the *meias laranjas* the remainder of the soil does not move, even by sudden slips separated by long periods of stability, for such movements would give easily identifiable colluvial lenses of the lower, red material within the upper, yellow horizon.

This situation results in the first place from the great effectiveness of chemical decomposition, which is incomparably more active than in the temperate zone. Subaerial weathering works under optimum conditions of warmth and humidity, so that in the space of a generation, fresh rock can undergo significant alteration. Fragments of white mica have been transformed into clay in about 10 years in a quarry in Madagascar, according to S. Henin. The stones of augen-gneiss that form the building of the Departamento Nacional da Produção Mineral in Rio de Janeiro, which was built about 30 years ago, show a significant removal of iron from the biotite which has covered all the gently sloping ledges with rust. Similar crystalline rocks used in the foundations of the monuments of Parati about 300 years ago, already show the first signs of the formation of clay minerals.[1] The hardest rocks, syenites of Brazil and Madagascar, are striped with lapies formed by solution, as on limestone. The quartzitic ridges themselves, rising above the forest, have a form which is both finely chiselled and smoothed in contrast with the hogsbacks of the same rock found in dry climates.

Among other factors which have sometimes been invoked to account for the impressive speed of chemical decomposition is the pH of rainwater. Certain authors suggest it contains a much greater quantity of nitric acid derived from thunderstorms; but the most recent statistics published in *Tellus* have given results which do not suggest extreme values compared with those for the temperate zone.

The climate also works through the intermediary of vegetation, which through its ability to colonise bare rock creates a soil on much steeper slopes than in temperate regions. On the northern flanks of the Agulhas Negras, one can see forest colonising syenite on slopes

---

[1] This is if we assume that the builders did not use a rock which was already weathered to some extent.

which reach 70°. As in all climates, the attack on the rock begins with the incrustation of lichens, but very quickly plant colonisation takes on a different aspect: this is the xerophytic vegetation characteristic of the caatinga (especially the cacti) which is adapted to dry soil conditions. At this stage there will also be several epiphytes which normally cling to the trunks of the tropical forests, but which will find adequate humidity even on a very steep rocky slope, as a result of the frequent rains or fogs. Their decomposition provides a thin layer of soil which is then utilised by other vegetation, and so on.

The volume of plant material in a humid forest is two or three times that found in a temperate forest, and so provides, as it decomposes, two or three times more carbon dioxide and other organic acids. The direct effect of this vegetation, and doubtless that of organic acids also, can however only work on slopes which are so steep that the soil is thin. Elsewhere there is only one factor of importance, the total amount of carbon dioxide produced by decomposition. One ought to add, hypothetically at least, the action of certain bacteria. On the other hand, where rainfall exceeds two metres (80 inches per annum) the amount of water moving as percolation, and in addition as surface run-off, is also two or three times more important than in the temperate zone (over 700 mm = 27.5 inches).

It is not possible to say whether tropical chemical decomposition is qualitatively, or only quantitatively, different from that in the temperate zone. This raises the question of laterisation which we can only touch on here. The soils of warm, wet climates are characterised by the large-scale production of kaolinic clays, which in other climates are only found sporadically, mixed with or juxtaposed with other types of clays (illite, montmorillonite, etc.). In the tropics there is always a horizon strongly enriched with hydroxides, often including free amorphous or crystallised alumina; there is certainly an enormous difference of degree from podsolisation. At the contact with the fresh rock, clays of the illite type show that weathering passes through a stage similar to that in the temperate zone. But this zone of separation draws attention at the same time to a completely new feature: the presence of gibbsite within rock which is hardly altered to clay at all. In general, desilification is a characteristic of soil development in hot and wet climates, as is apparent from the higher content of silicon dioxide in river waters (15–30 mg/litre). What role does vegetation play in lateritic weathering? Its role is certainly not a clear and direct one (contrary to the opinion of J. Ehrart). Kaolinisation and the appearance of gibbsite occur right at the zone of contact, several tens of metres below the surface.

In the search for a specific factor capable of explaining laterisation, it has been thought that bacteria might play the role of intermediaries in speeding up the chemical reactions (and this up to great depths where silico-bacteria can be found); laterisation would then be a type of 'tropical disease'.

The processes of transport on the slopes are relatively less active, although having a higher efficiency than those of the temperate zone. Transport in solution which works on any slope is appreciable, and remembering the intensity of drainage one may estimate that it is three times that of the temperate zone in a crystalline massif; but measurements by Freise suggest that it represents little more than a tenth of the total loss of material.

Wash is more active than in temperate forest for several reasons: (1) the ground flora is less well developed (as a result of the very low light levels); (2) the humus layer, masking the mineral soil, is thinner; (3) the showers are more concentrated.

However, according to studies by Rougerie in the Ivory Coast, diffuse wash, affecting the whole of the slope, only carries silts or very fine sands. But at the foot of large trees, the flow is concentrated (as can be studied, for example, in the area of virgin forest on the island of São Sebastião). The water runs down the branches to the trunk and unites into a considerable stream which scours the soil and carries away even the coarsest sand. Trees about 30 years old can give hollows some 15 cm deep. In secondary forest, the ground layer of the understorey is much less continuous. The effectiveness of wash thus varies largely with the permeability of the soil, which itself depends partly on the type of clays which are more or less hygrophilous (kaolin is relatively permeable), but especially on the state of the iron. Often the iron will cement distinct aggregates, giving the lateritic clays a porous texture, for example in the Congo.

The saturation of the soil by heavy rain leads to flow which is particularly active at a depth of 50 cm, below most of the roots. These have a relatively shallow position, especially when compared with the great depth of the soil. They have given up the attempt to reach fresh rock wherever the slope levels out, and draw their nutritive material from the detritus of the forest itself, substances more easily obtained the nearer the roots are to the surface. But these slow movements only affect the upper part of the layer of decomposed rock. On moderate slopes in Africa, as in Brazil, there is always a reddened, extremely compact zone, which is rich in clays and de-hydrated oxides of iron, protecting the unconsolidated sands beneath.

The removal of dissolved substances by percolating water leads to creep phenomena. On the other hand, saltation due to the fall of dead trees is probably less effective than in virgin temperate forest, for the dead trunks are held up by lianas; exceptionally strong winds are needed if they are to be brought down. Finally, the activity of wood termites moves a significant quantity of mineral soil which sooner or later falls back again farther down the slope. For certain authors, saltation caused by termites would even be the cause of the yellow, mobile, colluvial horizon. The termites would have removed from the altered horizon the silt and clay to build their mounds, leading to the separation of the larger fragments, especially the stone-line. This hypothesis certainly accounts for the fact that in Brazil the stone-line reaches the summit of the *meias laranjas*, where it clearly cannot be derived from lateral transport.

The only alternative hypothesis is that of a downward migration of the relatively heavy material to the base of a loose mass of low density. This hypothesis has been upheld by Laporte, who has studied an excellent section along a railway line in the Congo. However, the arguments which he advances are questionable: according to him the detritus would descend in a perfectly vertical line, although in all cases which we have examined, horizontal migration is evident. Further, the regularity of the line which forms the lower limit of the loose material must be explained; perhaps it results from an indura-tion of the red horizon through the vertical movement of iron, so that often the iron content of yellow and red horizons may be similar.

It has also been suggested that colluvium on the top of isolated hills could develop from a system of concave slopes from which the *meias laranjas* might have been created. This process may well ac-count for a cover on outliers that are immediately adjacent to a major escarpment such as that of the Serra do Mar, but not for those which are several miles away from it. On the latter, mass movement has long since removed every trace of any earlier colluvial cover.

Landslides play a major role and are characteristic of the system of erosion found on slopes exceeding 40°. These are due to the funda-mental fact, which has already been noted, that a fine-textured soil extends below the root zone on slopes between 40° and 60°, a result of the irresistible colonisation by forest vegetation. These landslides have been noted in virgin forest in all the tropical humid regions (e.g. New Guinea, Africa, Brazil). They were studied in great detail in

Hawaii (White, Wentworth). Eighty per cent of the landslide scars have a slope of between 42° and 48°. The upper limit is due to the fact that on steeper slopes the soil only rarely attains the necessary minimum depth of 60 cm. The largest scars visible are 150 metres in length and striations and grooves are visible at their base. The loss of material calculated by Wentworth represents an annual layer of material of the order of 0.9 mm. Freise has obtained values of the same order of magnitude on granitic rock in Brazil. These two authors have developed a cyclic theory according to which slope failure is periodically favoured by an automatic regression of the vegetation. This regression would result from the impoverishment of the soil which would lose all nutritive material; this would lead to the automatic replacement of the forest by a herbaceous layer with short roots incapable of holding a thick soil. Following rather heavier rains than usual, the soil would slip *en masse*, exposing fresh rock and so reinitiating the cycle. One can object that according to this theory the forest would be likely to destroy itself on the more gentle slopes where the loss of nutritive material could not be offset by landslips exposing fresh rock and that consequently the forest could not re-establish itself. In fact the permanence of extensive forests covering plains and hills alike would seem difficult to deny, at least on a historic scale; indeed, Freise assigns a length of 400,000 years to his cycle, but in that case it would not have much morphological significance.

Landslips are more or less favoured by the type of rock, which even in tropical humid climates influences the type of decomposition. They are more frequent where there is a sharp contact between the fresh rock and the decomposed clays (as is true of basalts), and where the products of decomposition have thixotropic properties.

The relative paralysis of linear erosion is evident from the many cascades, and in particular from their distribution. Together with the thick soils this is, to a European observer, the most significant feature of the morphology of a humid tropical area. With the exception of certain postglacial falls, the familiar setting of waterfalls outside the tropics is that of gorges with rock sides, where the bed is incised over a considerable length into the outcrop of the resistant rock. The two types of fall found in tropical humid regions are very different. In sedimentary structures the river arrives tranquilly on the brink of the cornice forming the edge of the hard rock, and falls precipitately with scarcely any incision. Similarly, in crystalline masses the fall merely covers the convex surface of a resistant core, the slopes above and at the cascade preserving a relatively gentle angle. In the two cases, it is commonly observed that the bed may be broader at the fall than in the quiet reaches above and below, precisely the opposite state of affairs to that found in the temperate zone (fall of Imbuí, near Teresópolis). These falls are very common. It appears that the obstacle to fluvial incision provided by these old rocks (and their cover) is due more to climatic causes than recent tectonic movement. Between the falls extend quasi-horizontal reaches, even at the foot of steep slopes. The explanations of this phenomenon are difficult to disentangle. They are due, it seems, on the one hand to the weakening of linear erosion in absolute terms, because the river is very short of pebbles, and also to the fact that the denudation of the valley sides is such a rapid phenomenon.

A well-established principle is that the river appears devoid of power, for it lacks pebbles to scour potholes. Even very steep slopes provide only a few rock fragments of suitable size. Crystalline rocks and massive sandstones supply the river with either large boulders or grains of sand, probably the result of the absence of frost to provide fragments of intermediate size. The few fragments which are made into pebbles break up very quickly into sand in the course of their movement. Quartz and quartzites constitute most of the large fraction of the alluvial material and are chiefly derived from erosion at waterfalls. Similar experiments made in the Congo, West Africa and Surinam show that these siliceous rocks have been worn into sands or very small gravels after transport of some 10 km downstream. If fresh, resistant rock causes a break of slope in the bed, the river has no tools to erode the rock over the section immediately above the fall where the flow is speeded up. Consequently, the typical convexity, that in temperate conditions extends several kilometres upstream of the break of slope, is hardly formed at all. To erode potholes at the foot of the fall, the river has only a few, new fragments, supplied by the impact of the falling water on any projections at the side of the fall where the outcrop of the resistant rock is small. If the outcrop is fairly extensive, the detritus provided by the slopes gives the river renewed erosional power. It must not be forgotten that even quartzitic or quartzose rocks have already suffered considerable comminution on the slopes themselves. Sections through the immobile part of the soil show that a thick layer (e.g. 10 cm) is broken up into rounded pieces of small size solely as a result of chemical decomposition, for it can be established that these fragments are strictly *in situ*. On the other hand, the area of outcrop of the resistant rock usually remains quite small precisely because the river is unable to incise itself into it. The very gentle gradient of the intervening stretches can be explained in the same way, for even steep granitic slopes provide the river with nothing more than very fine material.

Many questions still remain. One of the most delicate problems is the explanation of the rapid downstream decrease in size of fragments of siliceous rock. One theory has been suggested to account for this phenomenon in African rivers: the pebbles of quartz would decay by solution, ferruginous gels would be deposited in cavities, and these would be capable of breaking up the siliceous material by alternate drying and soaking. This theory requires an accelerated chemical decomposition in the river itself which leads to a difficulty: tropical waters are generally very acid and consequently quite unsuited for the solution of silica. The pebbles derived from such slopes must be studied more carefully to make sure that they have not already been rendered fragile by sub-aerial corrosion.

J. Tricart has suggested another phenomenon to explain the immunity of river beds. In the zone which is alternately covered and uncovered by the river a layer of manganese and iron will be deposited which has a protective effect. However, it does not seem that too much importance should be attached to this for it would suggest that one ought to find the low water channel sharply incised into a protected flood plain, and this is not the case.

On the other hand, it is incontestable that in truly mountainous regions (e.g. the massif of Tijuca or that of Itatiaia), the number of pebbles found at the bottom of the bed is sufficient to lead to erosion; waterfalls follow at such close intervals that there is little chance for much wear of the pebbles. However, they do not cut far into the mass of hard rock. The large torrent forming the cascade of Maromba is only incised a few decimetres while a temporary tributary that only flows for a short time immediately after a major rainstorm is deeply incised across a more gentle slope. This is due to the phenomenon of differential decomposition. Unlike conditions in the temperate zone, chemical composition precedes linear erosion to some extent, even in mountainous country. However, for reasons still unknown, a few crystalline cores are untouched by such decomposition and, as we shall see, are incipient sugar-loaves. When even a major stream meets these cores it merely flows over them. The enlargement of the bed which occurs is due to the fact that lateral erosion works much more easily in soft rocks which have been very deeply decomposed on each side of the stream. These give a relatively gentle, rather than a rocky, valley at the fall, to the surprise of the European. Further, if the channel is relatively narrower away from the fall, it is because the river there generally follows a zone of weakness (e.g. the fall of Teresópolis). The broadening of the channel necessarily causes a decrease in erosive power.

It is necessary to go further and ask if this apparent weakness of the river in relation to domes of hard rock might not be due to the fact that often it has only occupied its present position for a short time, as a result of lateral movements of its course. It may be imagined that by lateral erosion in the rotted rock on both sides, or by a type of auto-capture, the river comes to wander round the cores of hard rock, keeping to the weaker zone on one side or the other, or at least to that part of the resistant rock which has been deeply decomposed. All these falls would therefore form epigenetic phenomena, super-imposed from the deep soil: in brief, epigenesis would be the origin of these anomalies much more than the weakness of mechanical erosion.

More generally still, although we are forced to relegate the tectonic factor to a second place in explaining the number of cataracts where the disposition of initial faults and folds is poorly known, we must not go too far in this direction. It must not be forgotten that chemical decomposition may obscure the structures of an area very rapidly. None the less it remains true that, while in the temperate zone vertical incision often precedes to some extent the evolution of slopes, this is not so for the tropical humid zone (nor the arid zone).

The ideal cycle in a tropical humid climate

These principles will now be used to construct the cycle of erosion in a tropical humid climate.

In the whole of the tropical humid zone, rock outcrops are rare, to the despair of the geologist. The majority of the cycles of erosion evolve without passing through the phase of true youthfulness, for the incision of talwegs has not been rapid enough to disturb the plant cover.

If we are to consider a complete cycle of erosion, the first problem which arises is that of the circumstances which would allow the emergence of rock slopes, despite the rapidity of chemical decomposition and the ineffectiveness of linear erosion. It is, in fact, a most

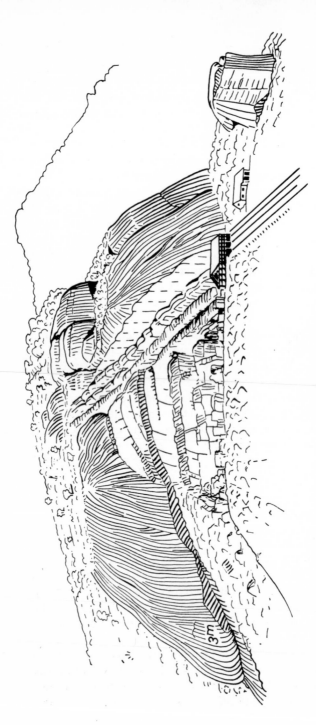

Fig 11   Residual relief of the slopes of the Serra de Bangu, Rio de Janeiro (quarry of Senador Camará). On the left a half-dome, formed by curved granitic layers. The quarry shows their structure with an enormous lenticular scale exceeding three metres in thickness which the quarrymen have succeeded in removing. The block on the right is separated from the half-dome by a series of closely spaced sub-vertical shatterings along the line of which a section has been removed. Its lower part has undergone subaerial rounding. At the bottom right an enormous block, detached along curved joints, has slipped to the lower part of the slope where the network of joints is closely spaced and where chemical decomposition is deep

unusual occurrence which depends to a varying extent on the phenomenon of differential erosion.

Sugar loaves

In the preceding section we were concerned only with perfectly homogeneous rocks. In fact this is a simplification even in the Serra do Mar. Some bare rock slopes are capable of appearing in the course of evolution of the cycle of erosion.

These slopes are associated with sugar loaves which are a phenomenon of differential erosion giving abnormally steep slopes. Their position in the landscape is almost always the same. At the foot of broad slopes differential erosion does not seem to be active; these more or less elongated conical relief features appear isolated and follow a preferred orientation. They are more numerous in the coastal Serra, where the process of dissection is more advanced than in the Serra do Mar, but in both cases the process appears to be the same.

Even the outline of the relief is proof that we are concerned with a process of differential erosion, as has already been noted by Brajnikov. On the flank of the massif of Tijuca (*sensu lato*) are to be found all the intermediate stages between bare egg-shaped areas interdigitated with large forested masses and completely detached sugar loaves. Exhumation is evidently favoured by a sharp contact between a deeply kaolinised zone and the completely fresh rock of the rounded cores. The details of the topography of this unusual relief leads to the same conclusion. This relationship is particularly noticeable on the south and east flanks of the Cocvado, where the morro of Dona Marta is half detached, and on the north slope of the massif of Tijuca, where the remarkable sharpness of the peak of Grajaú breaks out of the broad wooded slopes. For another example we may cite the *morro* of Nova Cintra, a strongly asymmetrical hogsback which ends on its northern edge in a vertical cliff below which are gentler slopes. These slopes extend to the summit of the hogsback on the western part. Taken as a whole the profile is that of a faulted anticline in a limestone area. As this is clearly not a recent fault, the escarpment can only be the result of differential erosion; it is in fact unthinkable that the retreat of steep slopes parallel to themselves from a talweg would give this asymmetrical profile and this rectilinear outline. This differential erosion works in the interior of a leptynitic gneiss.

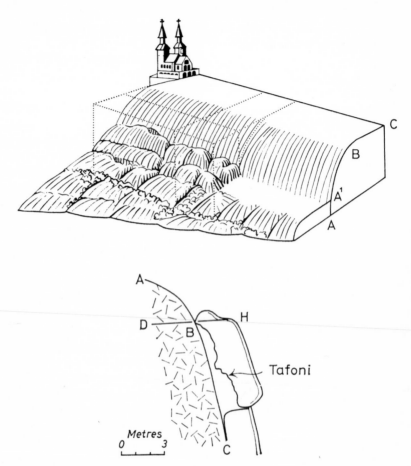

Fig 12   Granitic inselberg of the Nossa Senhora da Penha, Rio de Janeiro (part of the north slope). The rectilinear joints are very widely spaced, the sub-vertical joints being gently rounded so that they are sometimes difficult to distinguish from the rounding resulting from subaerial weathering. However, protected by a hollow, the convexity which is due to superficial exfoliation is still visible in A¹B, whereas BC and AA¹ represent the form of the joints. Below is a detailed section of the south slope. An enormous block formed between two sub-vertical and two sub-horizontal joints is in course of being detached by gravity. Its internal face is sculptured by tafoni

The principles which control this differential erosion are obscure and this is not the place to go into them too deeply. The contrast in resistance to erosion within the gneiss is as great as that between Urgonian limestone and marls. We may note that differential erosion depends in part on the type of gneiss. Biotite gneiss, which often occupies a synclinal position in the large vales separating sugar loaves, behaves as a relatively unresistant rock, the biotite being the first mineral affected, in monuments as in nature. The soils which overlie it are equally distinctive, coloured a violent red throughout almost all of their considerable thickness. But this petrological factor is probably only secondary; broad depressions such as that of the suburb of Leblon or that of the central part of the town coinciding respectively with augengneiss (which includes in fact the most resistant type of rock) and with biotite-free gneiss. The study of many quarries, as for example on the southern slopes of the Cabritos, has shown on the other hand that sugar loaves coincide with masses poor in joints, particularly vertical joints, whereas all the low hills without rock slopes, such as the Morro da Saudade, are scored by a closely-packed network of joints. The axes of the large depressions separating the lines of sugar loaves coincide with fractures, as is shown by the occurrence of veins of diorite or green stone; these are even more numerous than is indicated on the geological map of A. Lamego. Naturally these vales are not formed merely by the erosion of these narrow veins which are formed of rocks that are in any case fairly resistant to chemical decomposition. In addition to this large-scale shattering, which is clearly seen in the quarries, there is also a very fine shattering at the scale of the crystals. This fact has already been noted in the notable work of Lamego (1938). Conversely, the thin plates of gneiss of the sugar loaf show that the felspathic crystallisation has occurred only slowly, so sealing many of the earlier fractures.

The preferred alignment of fracture-controlled valleys and the major sugar loaves clearly indicates a tectonic influence. However, except in the case of the Pão de Açúcar itself, where as Lamego has shown the augengneiss overrides biotite gneiss, there is no trace of differential movement along the line of joints. On the other hand if, to a first approximation, the alignments of the sugar loaves can be considered as belts which have escaped tectonic fracturing, we are left with the problem of the origin of the curved joints which bound these masses on two or three of their faces. The layers are too thick for them to be caused by thermal exfoliation resulting from an annual range that does not exceed 10°C. The hypothesis that they are the result of unloading following the erosion of several kilometres of rock, is open to the major objection made by A. Cailleux that the effect of tension resulting from this phenomenon must be almost exactly compensated by the effect of contraction deriving from the gradual lowering of temperature as the surface comes nearer to these deep rocks. Moreover, one cannot completely accept the idea of Brajnikov (1953) that sugar loaves are similar to structures developed in the course of granitisation of sedimentary gneiss. In fact, the curved

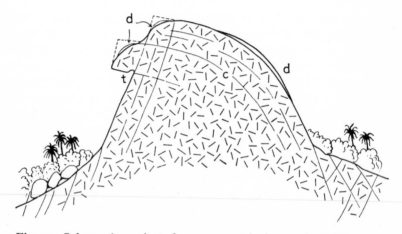

Fig 13 Schematic section of an asymmetrical sugar loaf. The core is formed by a mass poor in joints (curved joint c). These meet subvertical joints which determine the steep slope with the overhangs, with their interior faces covered with tafoni (t). On the more gentle slope, talus blocks derived from the overhang. These more gentle slopes are developed in a well-jointed rock and are covered with forest. At d, sub-aerial exfoliation

joints determining their outlines cut through the veins of all types of rock; not only the pegmatites, whose emplacement shows a certain harmony with the felspathisation of augengneiss, but also later veins, in particular those of aplitic granite.

 Whatever the reason, this intense differential erosion affects a zone at least several kilometres wide, whether on the flanks of the coastal Serra or at the foot of the Serra do Mar. With the exception of a few bare rock hills which rise some 50 metres above them, the extensive summit ridges of the Serra de Tijuca occur indifferently on gneiss of

all types and also across the lines of fracture. These transgressive surfaces must be due to the slowness of regressive erosion.

How do the exposed areas of rock exposed by regressive erosion
subsequently evolve? If we are to believe the work of Freise, they are
denuded with great rapidity, even more rapidly than the forested
slopes for which we have already given estimates. According to this
German chemist, a sugar loaf observed for 30 years showed a loss of
30 kg per square metre per year, which represents a layer of three
mm, three times the highest values noted in the Himalayas. Unfortunately the author gives no details of how his measurements were
made. He also quotes the evidence of workers on the cableway which
operates on the Pão de Açúcar, according to whom rock falls represent three kg per square metre, while the rock at the summit decomposed in 30 years to a depth of 45 cm. However, this last value
appears out of proportion to that observed on the monuments of Rio
de Janeiro, where in the same period decomposition has only penetrated one or two cm (even if one takes account of the fact that these
stones are appreciably polished and thus less vulnerable). These
extraordinarily high values appear incompatible with the fact that
the sugar loaves are the result of differential erosion, and incompatible with other measurements made by Freise suggesting that
streams would only remove an average thickness of 0.2 mm a
year from around the inselbergs. If the wear on the sides exceeds
that on the foot slopes, one would then find enormous accumula-
tions of detritus, and this is not the case. It is consequently necessary
to reconsider the quăntitative and qualitative study of these bare
slopes.

The most abrupt process is the fall of large blocks, usually bounded
on one side by curved joints, and on the other side by vertical joints.
This phenomenon is more common on the northern face of asymmetrical sugar loaves where vertical joints predominate (e.g. the
Morros dos Cabritos, do Cantagalo, etc.). The blocks begin to separate at the base and fall from overhangs on the upper part of the
sugar loaf. At the foot of each scar the detached blocks are still visible
which shows that they are not being rotted by chemical decomposition at the foot of the slopes. But they do not move towards the
talwegs; quite the contrary, as can be seen at the foot of the Morro da
Babilonia, where in a zone a few metres wide they dominate the
gentle hollows that lie on the piedmont. This proves that wear by
wash and solution on gentle slopes is relatively more rapid than the
retreat of the bare sides, and this is, in any case, the required condition

for their development by differential erosion. The fall of large blocks bounded by joints is completed by true exfoliation phenomena affecting layers of only a few decimetres or a few centimetres in thickness. Here too, weathering begins at the base, creating overhangs. More unusual is the case where the scales become detached on the upper part first, forming a type of flat-iron as on the north face of the Morro da Urca. Finally, granular disintegration is also active, cutting small pits in the form of tafoni, for example on the northern face of the Pão de Açúcar; these are frequently found in the shade of overhangs caused by the fall of blocks. These overhangs do not last indefinitely for, if they are not carried away by the fall of the upper part of the slope, they are worn by superficial exfoliation and by granular disintegration; the same is true of the vertical part of the layers delimited by the curved joints.

A quantitative estimate of the speed of these processes can be based on an examination of the proportion of the rock occupied by lichens. In fact, lichens occupy almost all the bare rock slopes except for a few white scars which are clearly seen; these correspond to the fall of certain overhangs or to the structural surface of those curved joint planes that have recently lost a scale. These scars represent a very insignificant part of the total surface. If we knew the time taken for lichens to colonise one square metre of the surface, we could derive some idea of the speed of wear of the bare rock.

It might finally be noted that it is not always easy to distinguish sugar loaves due to differential erosion and those which could be the result of dissection of the upper part of slopes. This is not surprising since there is no simple lithological distinction; these forms are identified almost on relief alone. The uncertainty is particularly marked for certain pillars of the Serra dos Órgãos, e.g. the celebrated Doigt de Dieu. It is likely that in this particular case one is dealing with an intermediate condition.

Thus we may suppose that the retreat of slopes on sugar loaves is in fact less rapid than has been suggested by Freise. It is not, however, negligible; one may not speak of an absolute immunity of steep slopes as in dry regions. By the later stages of the cycle of erosion, the complete levelling of sugar loaves is to be expected. A possible example of this may be found north of Niterói, where a quarry has cut into a small hill planed off at about 80 metres by the principal surface of erosion surrounding the Gulf of Guanabara. This mass of migmatite is particularly poor in joints; there is only a single system of oblique fractures about 10 metres apart. As this exceptionally hard mass does

not give rise to any feature, it seems probable that it has been levelled
in the later stages of a cycle of erosion.

Let us return to the case which may be considered the normal one,
a rock slope which results from the rapid incision of a river in the
shatter belt of a crystalline block. The margin of the Serra do Mar,
which results from a complex system of faults and monoclinal folds
(the initial structural picture is in fact too complex to reconstruct),
gives us a magnificent example. The phase of extreme youth in the
cycle is represented by the many valleys that exploit the lines of
fracture which are orientated NE–SW, and which probably accom-
pany a pattern of monoclines and faults. The retreat of steep slopes
occurs parallel to themselves according to the classical theory of
E. de Martonne. These slopes will acquire a considerable concavity
very quickly, only the upper part remaining rocky. However, independent of any polycyclic action, slopes with any very great area
(e.g. two km wide), which are concave in the upper part, will then
sub-divide into rounded, forest-covered ridges under the influence of
secondary talwegs fed by the concave drainage basin; this type of
topography is also common in temperate mountains. The upper rock
slopes degrade principally by rock falls, which originate from closely-
spaced joints formed parallel to the principal fault. But these blocks
are stopped by the trunks of the forest below and only move farther
on when individual trees die. Certainly exfoliation and granular
disintegration will be fairly active (and will be examined in more
detail later), but the general concavity and the absence of true talus
show that there must be an equilibrium between this weathering of
the blocks and that of the slopes immediately below. The lower slopes
are also divided into two parts: (a) the upper part with a slope
between 45° and 65°, which is dominated by landslips of the type
studied by Freise; the speed of displacement being practically in-
stantaneous, the slopes retreat parallel to themselves; (b) the more
gentle slopes, which pose major problems in the removal of this large
mass of detritus. On these more gentle slopes is found the soil sequence we have already described; a yellow colluvial horizon and a
lower horizon which has been constantly weathered but which is
immobile. The relative thinness of the colluvial material indicates
that there is almost a state of equilibrium because the thickness of the
moving soil increases very slowly down the slope: almost all the
detritus provided by the upper slopes is removed. It would seem that
there must be two different processes at work. On the rounded spurs
occur flow phenomena (wash and creep), and since the surface area

between each contour increases downhill, and the slope is convex, the thickness of colluvial material increases only slowly downhill. The detritus that comes directly from the concave basins higher up is carried by the principal streams. In this respect there is no essential difference from what happens in temperate humid climates. It must merely be noted that the layers and boulders of rock derived from the upper part of the slope by free fall or by landslip break up in the course of their journey and do not reach the talweg, as a result of the rapid speed of chemical decomposition.

Such are probably the idealised equilibrium conditions. But in Atlantic Brazil, convergent evidence of a climatic crisis complicates the actual landscape. One notes, in particular, block flows in a matrix of clay, formed largely of syenites or diorites. The mixture of lithological material shows that the horizontal transport has often exceeded several hundred metres (massif of Itatiaia, massif of Tijuca, island of São Sebastião). These rocks which are poor in quartz always show a sharp contact with the clays of decomposition, which is the reason why they slip so readily. This is certainly true for mud flows which can move even on relatively gentle slopes, as is shown by the form of the tongues of part of the flow and the fact that they spread over valley bottoms at a fairly low angle. This would seem to indicate a temporary decline in the forest cover. Other evidence of disequilibrium includes the little alluvial cones at the mouths of secondary gullies which are clearly superimposed on the form of the ridges. They are, none the less, extremely important as an indication of the abnormal erosion that has followed the devastation brought by clearance for coffee estates.

The succeeding stage of the cycle of erosion is marked by the increase of rounded, largely convex, ridges. They evidently result from the fact that the upper part of the slope has retreated and has disappeared. One may ask why, in the course of the cycle of erosion, the convex slopes should reappear as a very important feature of the landscape. This phenomenon is not peculiar to Atlantic Brazil for it has been noted by J. Dresch over much of tropical Africa.

Despite their small size, these hillocks have a steep slope of the order of 30° or 35°, suddenly ending in an almost flat and very broad base; in the same way, the secondary valleys end abruptly upstream in the form of a cirque. This phenomenon, which particularly impressed E. de Martonne, appears peculiar to tropical humid climates. There is no knick as in dry climates, but a concave junction with the talweg which is much steeper than those found in temperate regions.

Undoubtedly the frequent, virtually complete, absence of a concavity at the base of these convex slopes can sometimes be explained by alluvial deposition, as in the Paraiba valley in the neighbourhood of the Bay of Guanabara. Allowance must also be made for colluvial accumulation caused by a climatic crisis. This undoubtedly plays a large role in the African landscapes described by Dresch. The lack of surface drainage could not be accounted for without these disturbances of the equilibrium.

But the reasons are not lacking to explain why this solution may also be achieved in an equilibrium régime. It will first be remembered that steep slopes have a cover of fine detritus which can thus be moved across very gentle slopes. In the *meias laranjas* there are often almost perfect hemispheres joined by cols scarcely higher than the talwegs which they divide. The system of rectilinear fractures from which these hemispheres are derived has been easily exploited, and chemical decomposition is so intense in the shatter zones that even in the cols the evacuation of detritus is almost as rapid as in the true talwegs.

This removal is the work of linear sources (springs) surrounding the hill and functioning after several and repeated rainstorms. These processes may form the main distinctive features of tropical wet erosion (G. Rougerie). These springs are drained by streams (*marigots*) with small drainage basins, but which have a large discharge during torrential rain. They may therefore have a large wetted section, and they cut into the fine material to achieve a gentle longitudinal slope.

It seems that erosion surfaces developed in a tropical humid climate are intermediate between peneplains, the probable end of the temperate cycle of erosion, and the juxtaposed flats or pediments which, as we shall see, are developed in dry climates. This results, in particular, from the intermediate form of the concave slopes.

In the course of cyclic evolution, it has been seen that the relation of the longitudinal profile to the valley sides does not evolve in exactly the same way as in the temperate zone. Except in those cases where quartzites are abundant, the profile of the river depends much less on the material brought by the valley slopes. By contrast it may present numerous irregularities related to the hardness of the rocks which are moved only slowly. Thus in a temperate régime the smoothing of the profile of the stream bed occurs long before the establishment of a state of equilibrium in relation to the load brought by the slopes; in a tropical humid climate this sequence is reversed.

Features of polycyclic relief

The junction between two successive cycles in a valley or between two stepped erosion surfaces has a very different form from that found in temperate climates. Since linear erosion is relatively ineffective in relation to slope evolution, the most recent cycle cuts back only slowly into the older surface and only a few kilometres downstream, the valley affected by the new cycle is broad and open; the incised valley is wider than it is deep. The corollary of this form is the sharpness of the break of slope that separates two successive surfaces of erosion, in contrast to the temperate zone, where the interfluves separating the valleys of the new cycle progressively become more gentle downstream. The break is sometimes so sharp that it is easy to confuse it with a dissected fault escarpment separating two fragments of a single surface.

The remains of old cycles are even more fragile in a humid tropical climate than in a temperate climate, posing increased difficulties in their correct reconstruction. Undoubtedly in a temperate climate, breaks in the longitudinal profile become smoothed very quickly, although the flats are preserved much longer. By contrast in humid tropical climates, the decomposition of the rock is so deep, extending below the level of the valley floors (crypto-decomposition), that the remains of the old maturely-dissected valley wear away very quickly. In the Rio area the ghosts of a series of epicycles occur, but it seems impossible to reconstruct their exact position and even their number; the range of error is around 50 metres. The evolution of the slopes is so rapid that it is particularly dangerous to use accordant summits as evidence of a former surface.

If the remains of undeformed surfaces are poorly preserved, this will be even more true where they have been tilted. In the old massifs of the temperate zone, the fossil surfaces of erosion play an important role. Their exhumation may be sufficiently perfect, and their preservation sufficiently good, for it to be possible to reconstruct a series of facets and so estimate the exact extent of successive stages of deformation. This is not the case in the deeply rotted crystalline masses of the humid tropics where the discordant overlying sandstones are often harder than the rocks beneath. A very slight tilting movement is sufficient to transform the old surfaces into a landscape of slow denudation, a labyrinth of hills and vales. Even if a subsequent wave of erosion attacks the whole area, a perched river can flow sluggishly across an area reduced to a few square kilometres, for as we have seen

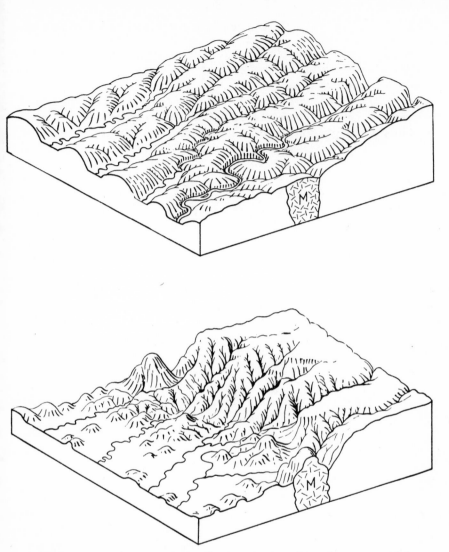

Fig 14 Landforms corresponding to the junction of two cycles of erosion. *Above*, a humid temperate; *Below*, a humid tropical climate. *Above*, the remains of the older cycle, profoundly eroded after rejuvenation, are now represented only by fragments of very modified plateau (on right). They pass progressively into long low ridges. The later cycle is only represented by broad mature eroded valleys (to left). In the centre a valley with incised meanders. A rather harder granite mass (M) gives only an insignificant feature. *Below*, a sharp contrast between the remains of the older platform with unrejuvenated valleys, and the already extensive levelling created by the second cycle (on left). The harder granitic masses give sugar loaves (M)

headward erosion barely precedes the rejuvenation of the valley sides. Characteristic features such as these appear in many of the highest massifs in Madagascar.

The only case where uplifted surfaces of erosion are well preserved is where they are protected by a ferruginous palaeosol, but as we shall see, this phenomenon implies a change of climate.

6 Erosion cycles in arid and semi-arid climates

General characteristics

As before we shall begin by defining the various morphogenetic conditions. The semi-arid climates are those where, on normal slopes and normal rocks, the cover of vegetation is discontinuous so that the mineral soil appears over an appreciable part of the surface. By this term normal is meant slopes of the order of 5° to 30° and rocks which are not particularly unsuitable for decomposition: granite, limestone or sandstones. (By contrast, in humid climates bare rock outcrops only on slopes steeper than 45°, and on even steeper slopes in tropical humid climates.) Seen from the air the landscape shows a scattered pattern of small shrubs, thickets, and clumps of grass, without any large areas that are completely bare.

In truly arid climates, the discontinuous vegetation is limited to a few suitable areas (valleys between the dunes, bottoms of wadis), the remainder of the ground being true desert. Such arid zones are relatively rare in the world: in particular, large parts of the Sahara, much of the Chilean desert, but all the other 'deserts' are, in practice, areas of semi-arid conditions according to the definition above. The erosional relief of true deserts is, in general, almost entirely derived from moister palaeoclimates, especially from semi-arid phases.

Two essential features appear in the landscape: (1) *The existence of broad surfaces, approaching a perfect plane*; these start suddenly below steep slopes and extend down to the talwegs. The French term *glacis* which is used to designate these plane surfaces is derived from the military tactics of the seventeenth century; it was the gentle slope which protected the wall of the citadel against cannonballs. The rival term 'pediment' evokes an architectural comparison: the two sloping lines like a low gable often found over the portico of a temple. This feature distinguishes the dry climates from all the other types of erosion found in the world, even when the cycle of erosion is almost complete. In all the humid climates there are always convex or concave undulations, shown on a map by sinuous contours. A map of an arid area shows contours that are straight lines over great distances. The first problem is to understand how these *glacis* or pediments develop; there is no equivalent in other climates for they have properties that are intermediate between those of a slope and a river bed.

(2) The second characteristic is *the sharpness of forms due to differential erosion.* Where there is an alternation of resistant and unresistant beds, even if the unresistant bed is as little as three metres thick, it is marked in the landscape by a depression dominated by a cornice. The slightest lithological difference is immediately apparent: a slightly harder vein in a granite, even if no more than a few metres wide, is expressed in the landscape by a narrow ridge which can sometimes be followed for miles.

In addition, a third feature is that *the hydrographic network is often endoreic.* There is also appreciable variation in the form of the hydrographic network according to the subtleties of the present climate, the succession of palaeoclimates, and the relief. When the hydrographic network is in equilibrium with the semi-arid climates, and provided that the relative relief is adequate, it is integrated over very great areas. By contrast, in arid climates the organisation of the drainage is very sketchy and one is dealing with a multitude of closed depressions of small size. One may define these concepts quantitatively on the basis of the average area occupied by a coherent drainage network. In arid areas, the order of magnitude is between 100 and 1,000 km^2; in semi-arid conditions 1,000 times greater. But two supplementary factors intervene: the relative relief and climatic change. In regions where the energy of the relief is very great, for example in the Ahaggar of the central Sahara the hydrographic network is fairly well developed because the available relief exceeds 2,800 metres. By contrast, in a very flat semi-arid area the organisation of the drainage is much more imperfect. Another factor is the succession of palaeoclimates. It often happens that, even in a semi-arid climate, the drainage net has been developed under a moister climate and that the drier phase only takes effect slowly. This disorganisation of the drainage operates in various ways and at quite different scales; from the ripples of sand on a slope, or the slight reversed slope of a solution pit which holds up wash, to a large dune barrier which is only occasionally breached by an important wadi.

*The processes—*1, *The agents of rock decomposition*

For a long time thermal variations have been considered the essential factor in the decomposition of rocks in dry climates. This problem has already been considered and we have seen that without the presence of water purely thermal decomposition cannot be very efficient.

Whenever the type of rock is suitable, granular disintegration predominates, often penetrating deeper than exfoliation. The surface of the scales is covered by a veneer which is often thinner than in tropical humid regions. It is composed of ferro-silicate solutions with a little manganese oxide. These solutions migrate through a few centimetres at the most, coming from within the rock and being precipitated on the surface by evaporation. Consequently on the internal face of the scale there are almost always signs of incipient chemical decomposition, which is the cause of the separation of the scale. Analysis of this internal fractured zone shows that the clay produced is of the montmorillonite type or of colloidal chlorite (inselbergs of Ahaggar and of southern Arabia in the Djeddah). It is known that these substances are very hygrophilous and so are able to cause important tension effects at the base of the scale after heavy rain.

The scale only remains intact if it is a fine-grained rock. In all other cases, granular disintegration reduces it to a sand before it reaches the base of steep slopes. In semi-arid climates this destruction is caused by a small clay content, or simply by the expansion of water trapped in fissures and the expansion of crystals which are themselves hydrated (in which case there is no sign of chemical decomposition).

In true deserts *Salzsprengung* appears, which in theory finds its optimum conditions of efficiency here. Dusts containing sodium sulphate and sodium carbonate are carried by the wind and precipitated on the slopes by rain. The crystals of sodium sulphate grow and so develop a pressure of 240 atmospheres and those of sodium carbonate 300 atmospheres. Under laboratory conditions, granite or grit slabs have been shattered in four months, by daily moistening when covered with a saline crust. In nature, this wetting would be the result of mists or light showers which are more frequent in deserts than might be imagined. The major cloudbursts carry away the loose grains, but temporarily arrest the growth of the crystals since these are dissolved. This process can be purely mechanical, but in those regions where the salt incrustation is long-lasting, it can be accompanied by the commencement of chemical decomposition of the felspars; certainly this is suggested by laboratory experiments. The fact that sandstones are, in general, more resistant than granites presents a difficult problem. This may be a matter of optimum porosity, but while chemical decomposition is naturally almost inactive in the sandstones, it may function alongside *Salzsprengung* in granites and so explain their weaker resistance. Experiments show that while schists are attacked by *Salzsprengung*, they are just as sensitive to temperature variations when wetted by distilled water.

Some of the most picturesque forms in which granular disintegration occurs are the features known as tafoni. An overhang will provide shade where water is retained. This is increased at night by dew. The process is extremely active in the Ahaggar where the black veneer is often attacked, and in the American West, where Bryan has noted an inscription dated 1874 which is already partly worn away. By contrast, limestones are evidently resistant to these types of disintegration while at the same time conditions are very unfavourable for solution, given the absence of water, the high temperatures and the almost complete absence of organic matter. This is why, along with quartzites and crystalline rocks of low porosity (veins, etc.), they almost always form the significant relief.

2, *Agents of Transport*

The arid system of erosion is marked by the overwhelming importance of two agents of transport on slopes: these are wash and wind; wash works in semi-arid climates, while in arid climates it gives place to wind. These agents of transport can of course only move detritus of small size: at the maximum sands or small gravels. But larger fragments can be carried by modes of transport intermediate between wash and the wadis: the muddy waters of sheet floods which occupy areas which are themselves intermediate between the steep slopes and the wadi floors. Wash begins by occupying small anastomosing runnels one or two cm across. The streams of water wind around clumps of isolated plants or pebbles which they are unable to remove.

Then, with a heavy rainstorm, a true sheet of water forms which can be as much as 20 cm deep in a basin only a few square kilometres in area. This sheet flood is itself loaded with clay or silt which increases its density. These agents of transport must carry some material much larger than sand. After a particularly powerful sheet flood it can be seen that pebbles as large as five or six cm in diameter have been carried along. Once the water is charged with a sufficient load of mud, pebbles as large as a man's fist can be carried.

Through these various transitions, one eventually reaches the true wadi, fed by a much larger drainage basin, tens of thousands of square kilometres in area. The true wadi, a temporary river, will flow very suddenly at the end of a cloudburst: it generally occupies a variable channel in a very broad bed. These migrations are caused by barriers of alluvial material which are formed at the end of each flood and which divert the course of the next flood; these may only recur at intervals of several years. Thus, like sheet floods, the wadi sweeps across considerable areas. There is no localised incision: because their existence is brief (little longer than the shower which causes them), there is no time for a channel to develop and denudation extends over the whole of the area affected. A wadi which rises in mountains lasts rather longer, a few days instead of a few hours. Its erosive effect is thus proportionately greater. These points are very important in understanding the origin of these vast pediments, the characteristics of which are intermediate between those of a stream bed and those of a slope.

The competence (that is to say the size of the detritus) and the capacity of transport of the wadis are considerable; blocks of several cubic metres can be moved. At the beginning of the flood, a crest of water approaches, moving at about 10 km an hour, and during the first stage lateral sapping causes erosion of the banks. At this stage, there is what amounts to a pavement of blocks at the base of the bed; these are derived from the mountains and prevent any incision; the wadi is overloaded. The upper waters are clearer and as they flow rapidly they undermine the banks wherever these are formed of soft rocks. The longitudinal profile of equilibrium has a steep slope to allow the removal of large debris of mountain origin, and so the river flows very fast. By contrast, during the second stage of the flood, all the material coming from the slopes and the rocks on the bed have already been removed; the water is no longer fully loaded and the river can now attack its bed. This is the time when the location of the river bed changes. After perhaps five or six years a new flood will begin by blocking the gaps which had been so formed. But the scars cut by lateral erosion after the preceding flood cannot be healed.

On the whole, agents of tranport on the slopes and fluvial erosion are relatively more efficient than the agents of rock disintegration and this is well shown by the wide extent of bare rock surfaces. One real myth must be exploded: the concept of an *ennoyage désertique* or over-whelmed deserts, which has been put forward by the distinguished geographer Gautier. He had been struck by the fact that one some-times sees inselbergs rising out of the middle of alluvial basins in the desert and he concluded that desert relief is shrouded under its own detritus as a result of the inability of linear erosion to remove this material. But relief of this type is not common and is restricted to alluviated interior drainage basins.

These processes and their relationships dominate the very distinc-tive cyclic evolution of dry areas. The essential problem is the development of pediments. The basic principle in their explanation seems to be that in a dry area there is no fundamental difference be-tween the movement of debris on the slopes and of alluvial material in the river beds. We have seen that wash and sheet floods are capable of carrying sands and small pebbles on slopes of $1°-4°$, but obviously they are unable to attack fresh resistant rock. Except in rare showers, water flows as small rills along runnels. Apparently all drainage tends to concentrate more or less automatically, but an opposing factor is the preferential development of vegetation along channels which are periodically soaked by water. The clumps of grass which develop then form obstacles which divert the rills; thus the rills are constantly mi-grating and are unable to develop even in soft rock. The slope of a few degrees on which wash is effective is precisely the same order of magnitude as that necessary for larger rivers if they are to be able to move blocks. Thus are realised the essential conditions for areal denudation. From this point of view there is a fundamental contrast with humid areas where the vegetation cover is continuous.

In these latter areas, a secondary talweg with a gentle drainage basin possesses a capacity of transport of a different order of magni-tude from that of the agents of transport on the slopes. The latter are obstructed by the plant cover, while this is broken by the channel of the stream (whether the roots be killed off by frequent submersion or whether in mountainous regions they cannot develop because of the rapid movement of alluvial material). Marked linear incision occurs. In tropical humid regions one sees such a minor stream cut through several tens of metres of decomposed rock to reach the rock *in situ*, giving a way through the forest and providing outcrops for the geologist. This advantage is moreover extended and automatically increased by the presence of springs concentrating the ground water, itself a function of the thickness of the soil. Thus the relationship between a minor stream and the vegetation are exactly inverse to those we have noted in arid regions.

Further, the slope of the minor stream, fed by a catchment of small extent, is of the same order of magnitude as that of the main stream, at least where they are in equilibrium, but for very different reasons. Bare rock does not outcrop in the main stream-bed, any more than in the minor stream, except perhaps for a few quartz veins, and the average size of the alluvium is small. Thus one can appreciate the fundamental contrast in a humid climate between slopes on the one hand and the whole of the drainage system on the other, a contrast which is expressed by a sinuosity of contours and by the constant superiority of linear erosion over areal denudation.

Stepped planation surfaces and pediments

If observation shows us that there exists a mode of transport and areal erosion on plane surfaces at the foot of slopes, we must now explain why these plane surfaces should exist (apart from the simple depositional piedmont forms).

The cycle leading to the development of these plane surfaces must necessarily proceed through linear incision and the development of a longitudinal profile of equilibrium. The latter, approximately stabilised, then acts as a base level for the areal erosion which removes weathered material from the slopes. The valley widens, preserving a gentle cross-profile, the slopes retreating so long as the detritus can be moved across them.

Planation surfaces on crystalline rocks

These considerations apply to the interpretation of the evolution of the first type of planation surface. This is developed on resistant rocks which are fresh but, as they are crystalline rocks, they disintegrate easily into grains. The term pediment can be reserved for these features. Wash, either in rills, or as a sheet fed by a basin of a few acres, is able to move the sand even on gentle slopes, particularly as the steep slopes above the glacis produce detritus only slowly. These steep slopes also provide little in the way of large material. For example, large boulders of granite cannot slide in the absence of any lubricating material. Once the slope declines below the angle on which the grains are in equilibrium, they can only be moved by wash, as they are freed by weathering. This action is slow, particularly on steep slopes where run-off is rapid. Conditions for weathering are most favourable on the glacis itself as a result of its more gentle slope. This tends to establish an automatic equilibrium, the slope of the glacis decreasing over the whole area of its surface because the crystalline rock there breaks up more quickly. In general, the wash that occurs is more than adequate in relation to the quantity of sandy material produced, which explains why the 'soil' remains thin with large subhorizontal rock slabs subject to exfoliation. However the slope cannot decrease indefinitely, for the sand would tend to accumulate and so exceed the transporting ability of the wash. Any marked temporary excess in the transporting capacity of the wash is expressed by exhumation of the bare rock; that is to say, in the absence of a reserve of water, by a slowing up of the disintegration of the latter. This is a supplementary reason in explaining the automatic paralysis of any concentration of drainage.

The residual relief with steep slopes which dominates these erosion surfaces on crystalline rocks belongs to two very different categories. These Inselgebirge or Inselbergs (according to the extent of the relief considered) can result from the retreat of steep slopes parallel to themselves. But they can also be formed from more resistant rocks which are resistant to attack in semi-arid or arid conditions; then the planation surface ceases to extend or lower itself when it reaches its cross-profile of equilibrium.

This distinction is straightforward when one is dealing with distinct lithological categories, and where it is possible to compare geological and topographical maps. It becomes much more delicate where there are extensive outcrops of granite or gneiss. Their recognition then depends essentially on a study of the relief itself. When the disposition of the residual features faithfully follows the outline of a dendritic drainage pattern, the interfluves decreasing regularly downstream, it may be supposed that one is dealing with the first case. The inselbergs then deserve the name of 'Fernling' or 'inselberg of position' because their exceptional altitude is the result of their distance from the main streams. If on the other hand the pattern of the relief is chaotic, groups of inselbergs being situated towards the centre of the drainage basin close to the principal river, one must infer differential erosion, and one is dealing with a 'Härtling' or 'inselberg of durability' (fig 15).

One major group of rocks presents no such problems. Very fine grained rocks (aplites), or those showing two stages of emplacement or consolidation (rhyolites and veins of all types), are never levelled by planation surfaces whatever may be their chemical and mineralogical composition. These rocks are very resistant to disintegration, apparently because they are impervious. This lower porosity results in part from the fact that these rocks have very few joints, as their consolidation postdates the last phase of tectonic deformation. One

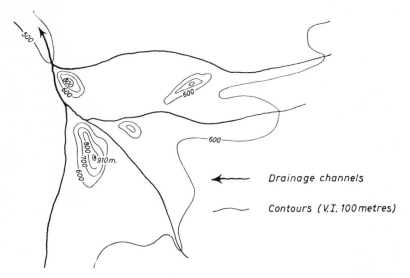

Fig 15   Diagram showing the situation of an inselberg in resistant rocks

must add that differential expansion of fine-grained rocks by variations of temperature is very much less than that affecting a coarse-grained rock. Finally, as a result of the smoother surface, rain water and saline dusts brought by the wind adhere to the rock less easily.

It seems that small bathyliths should be placed in the same category as long as these were emplaced slowly and consolidated into one mass not far from the surface. The largest example is the massif of Brandberg in southwest Africa which rises 1,500 metres above the neighbouring erosion surfaces and which has penetrated as far as the Karroo Beds. The 'younger granites' which pierce the old African shield almost always form relief features, as do the syenite massifs of Madagascar and Brazil.

In the majority of cases it is very difficult to explain the unequal liability of granitic and gneissic masses to granular disintegration. We shall limit ourselves to a description of a few types of inselberg and their relation to their neighbouring planation surfaces. The outline of the inselberg is determined largely by the pattern of its joint planes.

The inselberg koppies

Here the granite is cut up by a system of horizontal and vertical joints, which are generally an even distance apart, typically about a metre. These joints determine the stepped appearance that gives these inselbergs the appearance of a castle, as well as their sharp contact with the pediment. These steep slopes degrade directly by granular disintegration without passing through the stage of exfoliation and at a fairly rapid rate, for the Neolithic veneer has completely disappeared.

Boulder inselbergs (tors)

These are essentially a pile of rounded blocks in equilibrium on a substratum that often shows signs of clayey decomposition. Their slope does not exceed 35°, which corresponds to the coefficient of limiting friction of the blocks. As a general rule, it seems that these rounded boulders are derived from cubes delimited by joints similar to those of castle-koppies. This development is produced by crypto-decomposition in a more humid climate than that of the present time and more favourable to clayey decomposition.

These two types of inselbergs vary greatly in size from a few metres to several hundred metres and they evolve by the retreat of slopes parallel to themselves. Indeed in the absence of any vegetation to protect the fine debris against wash, there is never any chance of a slope declining by the flow of encompassing fine material moving some of the blocks. The planation surfaces, as they develop, will consequently eventually plane them off entirely.

Domed inselbergs

In contrast to the rugged, and sometimes very broken, profiles of the preceding type, are the silhouettes of dome-shaped inselbergs. The slopes are formed by curved surfaces which are perfectly smooth and of variable inclination. They are often divided into three sections: a gently sloping platform near the base, then a steepening, followed immediately by a strongly convex summit. Each break of slope is marked by a line of joints. These inselbergs, with a relative relief which often exceeds 1,000 metres (In Ekker, Tesnou), are formed of several layers separated by joints, much like the layers of an onion. Essentially, the surface of the feature is parallel to curved joints separating layers which are one to five metres thick. These are broken here and there by bluffs or scars of a half to a few metres, usually in the lower part: these normally correspond to the breaks in the curved layers and occasionally to vertical joints. As in the sugar-loaves of tropical humid regions, weathering takes place in part by gravity (the fragments of the curved layers slip and tend to accumulate at the bottom of the flexures affecting the curved joints), and in part by meteoric exfoliation separating scales a few centimetres thick. These scales are not rigorously parallel to the curved joints and are capable of rounding the angles formed where two curved joints meet; thus the entire smooth, convex surface is not necessarily a result of the removal of one complete layer. These erosional processes are much slower than in the tropical humid zone. Since the Neolithic veneer was formed, most of the large blocks have not moved, and the subaerial scaling has only affected a relatively small percentage of the total surface (Ahaggar).

When the scales are composed of a rock which disintegrates fairly easily, the rectilinear blocks pass through the stage of corestones as they decay. In this way some inselbergs show curious structural features with a hemispherical profile surmounted by rows of blocks which are the remains of one or more higher scales. However, it is uncommon for their arrangement to be absolutely symmetrical, for the scales do not have constant thickness and pile up in juxtaposed lenses. But on other occasions, more or less vertical joints actually intersect the curved exfoliation surfaces, as seen on western face of the bathylith of In Ekker. The curved surfaces separate granite layers that are alternatively of fine and coarse grain. The granite layers are broken by micro-faults which vary their hade and which are largely orientated N.N.W.–S.S.E. (following the old structural trend) and, less often, at a direction at right angles to it. The layers with coarse grains weather more easily and are sculptured by tafoni. In contrast, the fine grained layers have more or less completely preserved their veneer. Finally a last combination is found where the spine of an inselberg is formed by a layer where the vertical joints are close-packed so causing it to break up into boulders. These tend to slide on the smooth, convex, exfoliation surfaces of the adjacent sections.

Domed inselbergs occupy an intermediate position between the true Hartling and the Fernling. Their shape is essentially of structural origin, as are the major variations in their profiles; on the other hand certain domes of large size coincide with small bathyliths. But several domes of small size indicate a retreat of steep slopes parallel to themselves, although slower than that of other types of inselberg.

The processes leading to the development of planation surfaces on crystalline rocks are still active today (that is to say they post-date the Neolithic veneer) on the Mediterranean margins of the arid zone. However here, coincident with areal denudation, there is the beginning of appreciable vertical incision by the talwegs. This, together with the largely bare state of the surfaces, shows that, at the present time, the equilibrium between the rate of decomposition of the rock and the agents of transport is unbalanced in favour of the latter. Inversely, the planation surfaces are sometimes invaded by surfaces of deposition composed of sand, showing that in some very recent period the rock broke up rapidly.

On these Mediterranean margins of the arid zone the development of a planation surface on crystalline rocks is extremely slow, only a few centimetres in 5,000 years even in the most favourable cases. This can be seen from the considerable area of veneer covering the greater part of the steep slopes and even the rock slabs of the pediments themselves. It seems that erosion finds more favourable conditions on the equatorial margins of the desert zone. In the Mediterranean margins, despite the fact that variations of temperature are more important, the chemical effectiveness of rainfall is weak because it falls in the cold season. In contrast, on the savanna margins, the summer rainfall is capable of far more effective action, even on the slopes of the inselbergs. As a result, the cycle of erosion evolves more quickly towards its final stage, which one may call pediplanation. In the end, in fact, pediments by cutting back will eliminate almost all the residual relief. But the equilibrium slopes are much more gentle than on the Mediterranean margins because, on average, the detritus is smaller.

It can be suggested without hesitation that the ideal bioclimatic conditions for the development of planation surfaces on crystalline rocks are the low thorn forests (thorn scrub) of which the Brazilian caatinga is one of the best examples. The average annual precipitation is much greater than in the semi-arid zone of the Mediterranean margins (400–700 mm compared with 100–200 mm). Certainly the evaporation is also heavier, but the water will first flow down the slopes before forming a temporary lake some distance below the pediment. Falls of as much as 160 mm in two hours may occur. These heavy falls are of little use to the vegetation, as they are extremely irregular from year to year. The total fall for one year may be as little as 150 mm. The precipitation is insufficient to sustain a continuous vegetation cover, especially one that produces a large number of leaves. The volume of decomposed organic matter produced each year is very small and as a consequence the mineral soil outcrops very extensively between the trunks of the small trees, the cacti and the stems of the thorn scrub. The occasional very heavy showers thus produce a wash with maximum morphological efficiency. The steep slopes show appreciable chemical decomposition, although this only gives rise to granular disintegration. Unfortunately there seems to be no quantitative data to support these apparently straightforward propositions.

Planation surfaces on sedimentary rocks

The origin of planation surfaces on crystalline rocks has been explained in relation to a contemporary semi-arid climate. More problematical are those surfaces developed in less resistant sediments belonging to more or less folded structures with alternating hard and soft beds. This is not the place to deal with the problem at length and we will restrict ourselves to a few comparative remarks.

The type profile of a scarp slope or a '*glacis de front*' includes the following elements: (a) a fragment of structural surface corresponding to the top of the resistant bed, perfectly exhumed; (b) a steep slope, sometimes almost vertical, including the scarp of the resistant bed and below that a varying extent of the underlying unresistant bed; (c) an upper surface with steep slope (25°–35°) cut into the unresistant bed. Here and there, it may be covered with a fairly thin sheet of talus derived from the upper resistant bed, and perhaps incised by gullies; (d) finally, the true pediment, a vast and absolutely plane surface with a slope between 1° and 5°. It is almost always covered (to a depth between 30 cm and one metre) with fragments eroded from the resistant cap-rock, with their longest axis between five and 15 cm. The main problem is to discover how the cap-rock is shattered and the fragments transported over the pediment. The sandstones, and in particular the limestones, that form these free-faces appear under present conditions to be almost completely immune to decomposition. The fragments carried across the footslope are, on the other hand, of the size of a man's fist, and exceed the transporting ability of the sheet wash. In Africa at least, these pebbles are completely patinated, proving that they are no longer moving.

The almost vertical nature of the upper, steep slope is to be explained, not by the vigour of linear erosion, but by sapping phenomena caused by the easy erosion of the unresistant bed. It seems that there could be a rhythmic evolution. The upper resistant bed is almost immune to subaerial evolution, while the underlying unresistant bed is eroded much more actively on the upper part of the pediment by wash and in particular by gullying. These gullies result from a concentration of the drainage which can take place more easily than on the lower pediment because, as the water is flowing more quickly, it does not encourage the growth of vegetation which, as we have seen, tends to colonise rills developing on the less inclined pediments. By this process an almost vertical slope is formed. Solely as the result of gravity, a section of the face of the cap-rock shears away, often along the line of a joint. The large blocks accumulate on the lower part of the slope; their angle of equilibrium is of the order of 35°. This process can continue as long as the free-face is sufficiently high.

There now begins the slow comminution of this fallen material by weathering, under more favourable conditions than on the free-face of the intact bed. The large material gradually breaks up, while at the same time it slides down the underlying soft rock which is not completely protected from wash. Thus the talus slope (*glacis de fragmentation*) tends gradually to become cleared of blocks. With this change, the attack on the lower bed becomes increasingly effective and the initial situation returns. Part of the old talus escapes this erosion and gives rise to peculiar projections in the form of flat irons, facing inwards towards the free face. But this cycle is undoubtedly very slow. It is only capable of acceleration in climates where sudden rainstorms soak the unresistant rock, so that where the texture is suitable, flow occurs.

It is important to explain the rapid transition from the talus slope to the pediment. Where the latter is swept by a wadi there is no difficulty. The wadi is capable of carrying the fragments of the resistant rock even across a gentle slope. Further it will enlarge the pediment by lateral erosion for it will readily attack the unresistant bed, conforming to the ideas of Johnson (a process that cannot occur where wadis cross crystalline terrain). This lateral sapping is naturally favoured by the presence of a pavement of large fragments of hard rock which are only rarely moved. That such a process is very active can be seen from the small, very distinct, river cliffs found on these pediments.

But most of these signs of planation are not limited to the surface of a fan. Certainly a series of adjacent fans can be imagined, each swept through a full 180°. A few examples of this are known; but, in this case, deposition is much more significant, and along the change of angle at the base of the slope the level of the pediment shows considerable variation (with depressions at the meeting-point of two cones). It is not possible to explain in this way the rigorously uniform pediments which extend the whole length of a slope, unbroken except by insignificant notches. In this case it must be assumed that the pebbles have been transported by a sheet flood with a much higher competence and capacity than the agents working on the talus slope.

The talus slope must clearly have a minimum width so that discharge reaches an adequate magnitude at its lower extremity. If the slope there decreases sharply, the discharge forms a much thicker sheet of water than on the talus slope, capable of forming a true sheet-flood. At the same time, the average size of the detritus decreases across the talus slope, as has been noted in north Africa and on the Karroo slopes studied by Fair. J. Dresch, suggests that this decrease of size can be due to a sorting process, only the smallest material being carried away. This would be very probable if the agent of transport were wash; but this is clearly unable to move slabs of limestone or sandstone which are chiefly moved by thermal creep or *soutirage*; under these circumstances their speed of movement depends very little on their size. It seems likely that the essential feature in the diminution in size is the fact that these slabs gradually break up as they are moved along.

The presence of a resistant cap-rock is needed for the formation of pediments in unresistant rocks, precisely because it maintains the large talus slopes where slow decomposition can occur and the run-off accumulates. These two convergent phenomena allow the carrying of fairly large fragments across a much more gentle slope.

In present conditions, much of the material lying at the foot of the talus slope cannot be moved, even by sheet flood. The transporting capacity of sheet-floods is higher when they include an appreciable mud content to increase the fluid density. The wadis of the arid American west acquire an enormous competence in this way, comparable to that of a glacier. The genesis of these mud-flows is very different from that of the periglacial climate. The flow does not derive from the saturation of a great thickness of soil or rock on the slope, but from the carrying by flow of a quantity of finely fragmented loose material. Under present conditions, as has been noted by J. Dresch, mud-flows have never been observed to arise on the slope independently of any concentration of the drainage pattern. It must be supposed that the cover of detritus found on the pediment cut in unresistant rock has been formed under a climate rather different from that of today; one with heavier showers, although too irregular to give rise to a continuous vegetation cover.

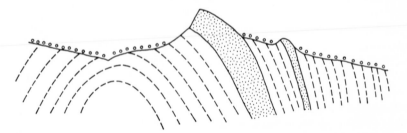

Fig 16   On the left a scarp-foot surface (*glacis de front*), and on the right a dip-slope surface (*glacis de revers*) in a folded structure

If one postulates an ideal climatic sequence for the development of pediments in unresistant rocks, the following scheme seems likely:

1   A fairly humid climate (perhaps even allowing the development of a continuous vegetation cover), the development of a true soil, and the disintegration, at least along river channels, of the hard rock.

2   The total quantity of rainfall decreases sharply and in particular becomes more irregular and concentrated into sharp showers. It is during this period that the pediments are formed, the resistant cornice, already partly weathered, retreating by loss of complete

slabs, or the removal of the fragments of the regolith already formed. The pediments are formed by lateral erosion by sheet wash. The sheet-floods are strongly charged with mud derived from the soils developed in the wet period, and so can carry large fragments of the resistant rock.

3 The drought increases: accumulation overtakes the extension of the pediment as a result of a decrease in competence and capacity of transport. The extent of this aggradation depends in large part on the amount of regolith on the resistant rock still untouched by erosion. This explains why only a few kilometres may separate bare pediments from true terraces.

4 Finally, the present drought is fully established. The soil formed during the humid periods is completely removed. The slopes cannot provide any more. Thus linear erosion is reinstated, incising channels into the pediment.

According to this scheme a large part of the cycle of erosion evolves during a period of climatic change.

The ideal cycle in an unchanging climate

During the Quaternary, much of the area now desert has experienced humid phases; these caused the arid areas to become semi-arid and the semi-arid areas to experience a sub-Mediterranean or savanna climate. Further, the major surfaces that occur in these regions and from which project most of the major inselbergs, may have been formed in the course of a tropical-humid phase in the Tertiary. Despite these uncertainties, it is desirable to suggest how a cycle of erosion might evolve in a fairly constant climate.

Semi-arid climates

An initial problem must be faced. Has linear erosion sufficient power to create steep slopes which are then capable of retreating parallel to themselves? A study of the behaviour of wadis, for example on the southern margin of the Atlas, shows that we are dealing with a very powerful mechanism capable of cutting into the hardest rocks. These incisions create steep slopes, on which disintegration is *ipso facto* paralysed; these slopes are extended at the base until the wadi is just able to transport those blocks that fall from the mountain slopes. The longitudinal profile of equilibrium is then achieved in the same conditions as for a temperate-humid climate. But the secondary streams are quite unable to keep pace. Over fairly extensive areas it is probable that the cycle never passes through the phase of youth; instead, especially in rocks liable to granular disintegration, planation proceeds through the intermediary of surfaces of slow denudation. In particular, granitic or sandstone relief decomposes in a multitude of basins, bristling with rocky knobs and sometimes separated by narrow gorges. This type of evolution inevitably occurs when erosion is attacking an area partly decomposed under an earlier climate.

As the steep slopes of the wadi sides retreat parallel to themselves back from the principal wadis, a pediment develops as soon as the main valley has attained its profile of equilibrium. This is strictly true where the steep slope provides only granular detritus, which has not passed through the stage of boulders (for example in the absence of joints). The profile of the pediment is then one which allows the movement of these grains as they are set free. The steep slopes dominating the pediment will, under these circumstances, never pass through the stage of equilibrium of the cross-profile. In fact their slope, which was formed by the incision of the main stream, subsequently remains constant and independent of anything that may happen to the main stream. In this type of evolution, significant 'inselbergs of position' may develop, but only where the interfluves between the principal talwegs are relatively narrow. Everywhere else, in the area of surfaces of slow denudation, inselbergs are necessarily 'inselbergs of durability', cores or bands of hard rock whose size increases towards the base as the gentle slopes of the surface of slow denudation are lowered. When the steep sides reach a sufficiently great size, there occur the conditions which allow the establishment of true pediments. The latter thus appear only at a late stage in areas of slow denudation. Further, barriers of hard rock can form local base-levels, giving a stepped appearance; this will not occur along the main wadis which are quite capable of cutting into even the most resistant rocks. In sedimentary structures with a significant proportion of unresistant beds, linear erosion is able to create steep slopes almost everywhere. Undoubtedly at the beginning of the incision the secondary streams will attack the upper, resistant bed only slowly, and the cross-profile remains open. But once the unresistant bed is reached, linear erosion works very rapidly leading to the enlarging of the cross-section and the development of steep slopes in the resistant bed; these often take the form of vertical walls (Monument Valley, Utah). In these conditions, the evolution of the pediment begins as soon as the longitudinal profile of equilibrium is established. But the

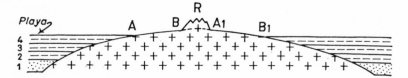

Fig 17   Evolution of pediment surfaces towards a dome. R—residual relief; 1,2,3,4—stages of successive aggradation; AB–A₁B₁—pediment

stream will incise itself quite rapidly once the pediment starts to develop. Previously it received large blocks directly from the cliffs of unresistant rock; once the pediment is formed, the stream will receive only those small fragments that can be transported across its gentle slope.

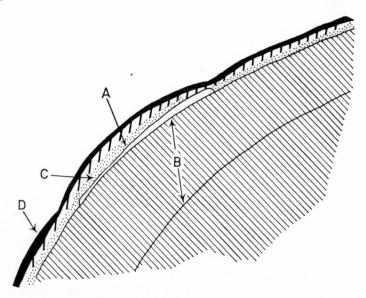

Fig 18   Section of the side of a granitic inselberg in course of exfoliation. A—scale undergoing swelling. B—curved joints. C—hydration and chemical alteration. D—veneer

We have already seen that the evolution towards general pedi-planation is much more rapid in tropical, semi-arid climates than in sub-Mediterranean climates, in particular because the latter are less favourable for chemical decomposition. Consequently while on the tropical margins the slope of the pediment is gentle from the first, it must undergo a series of modifications in the Mediterranean margins, for the size of the detritus increases after the earlier stages. Some American authors would invoke this phenomenon to explain the con-vexity of the pediments which become gentler as the residual relief is reduced. But the most gentle slopes of the youthful stage are them-selves buried beneath the depositions which fill the endoreic basins.

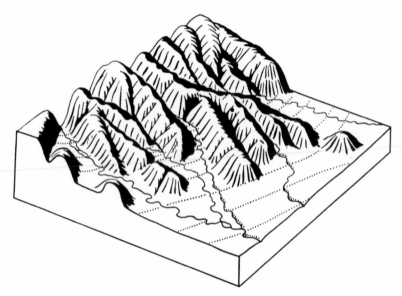

Fig 19   Development of a pediment by retreat of steep slopes paral-lel to themselves in a homogeneous crystalline rock. On the right an 'inselberg of position'

Following Davis, the ultimate form would be a vast, flattened dome without any real summit, such as the granitic domes of the Mohave Desert, although this idea is nowadays contested. It is interesting that phenomena of this type have never been observed in African pedi-ments which are always concave.

Among those features which pediplanation must eliminate in the Mediterranean margins are pediment-passes. These are cols formed by the meeting of two contemporary pediments which end in different base-levels; this difference of altitude would not occur if the profile of equilibrium of these surfaces were not so steep.

Even in optimum tropical conditions, the development of a pediment requires a long period of stability, first for the production of a longitudinal profile of equilibrium, and afterwards for the reduction, grain by grain, of the slopes.

This applies with even greater force along the Mediterranean margins. The pediments of the American south-west were developed over several million years at the end of the Pliocene and in the early part of the Quaternary under a climate that must have been slightly more humid than at present. They are today in a state of dissection and the sheet-floods normally flow across slightly-incised sheets of alluvium.

The arid climates

This system of erosion is characterised by the dominance of wind over wash, in so far as the transporting agencies are concerned, and by the inability of linear erosion to develop an organised drainage net of any size.

In these conditions the cycle of erosion attacking an uplifted surface never passes through the stage of youthfulness. The reduction of the initial surface takes place by a series of hydro-aeolian basins; these develop most readily in rocks liable to granular disintegration. This weathering results from the action of salts and occasional showers. Wind then raises the loose sands produced by this weathering. The basin deepens, for the wind is capable of lifting the sand over the enclosing slopes. This process cannot continue indefinitely, for the effectiveness of the wind is reduced as the basin deepens. There must exist a certain relationship between the width and depth of the depression. The widening of the depression is the work of wash. When the structure is suitable (sub-horizontal sediments capped by a hard bed), the hydro-aeolian basin is limited by a crenulate scarp indented by small gullies. But naturally this lateral erosion must not become too effective or the wind will be unable to remove all the material brought down by wash. It is true that the higher humidity resulting from the convergence of the rills favours granular disintegration, allowing the deepening of the basin. Nevertheless, this increase in humidity must not be so great as to allow the establishment of a plant cover that would fix the sands. In addition, the concentration of salts in the centre of the basin does not usually favour vegetation growth (while at the same time favouring granular disintegration). As a result, there is a very delicate equilibrium controlling the evolution of these hydro-aeolian basins, between granular disintegration resulting from the presence of water, the effectiveness of local wash and the strength of the wind. In general, the slow incision will work at different speeds in each basin. Pedimentation itself only appears in a transitory and local form, as a result of the wash on the margin of the basins. As a whole, the marginal scarps tend to retreat, but it seems unreasonable to suppose that the result of this will be the formation of

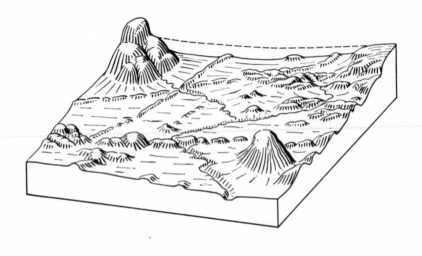

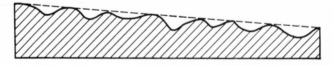

Fig 20   *Above*, a block diagram showing pediments and surfaces of slow denudation in a heterogeneous crystalline mass. There remain projecting intersecting veins, hills limited by curved joints of the general form of sugar loaves and an irregular pattern of projecting knobs. The wadis wander from basin to basin. *Below*, a section of a surface of slow denudation in a homogeneous rock developed from a cyclic surface (indicated by the broken line)

a broad, plane, uniform surface. This is particularly improbable in view of the ability of wind to lift material from below sea-level.

Naturally, all transitions can be found between the semi-arid and the arid cycles, depending on the relative importance of surfaces of slow denudation. These are not only the result of climatic factors. It is known that vast, extremely arid areas of the central Sahara are evolving in relation to an extensive hydrographic net which was cut in a more humid phase that extended throughout the area. On the other hand, in all climates the presence or absence of a true youthful stage in the cycle of erosion depends on the scale of the tectonic movements that initiate the cycle, and in particular the ratio between the height and area of the upraised block.

7 The cycle of erosion in areas subject to alternating wet and dry seasons or to alternating wet and dry climates

In the preceding chapters we have attempted to define the evolution of the cycle of erosion in hot climates which are almost constantly humid, and in dry climates with relatively brief humid phases. But the greater part of the tropical zone is subject to alternate dry and wet seasons of equal significance. In addition, much of this area coincides with that zone where, according to the evidence of palaeosols, humid climates and dry climates have alternated during the Pleistocene. This is particularly true of the larger part of western Africa. It is likely that variations on the scale of a millennium would be expressed by certain features in the systems of erosion and of pedogenesis. At the same time, in our attempt to reconstruct the evolution of the cycle of erosion in a constant climate, we have noted the effect of a succession of climatic crises, each capable of accelerating the processes of erosion.

Clearly this is a complex state of affairs. There is, in addition, a supplementary problem; the uncertainty over the nature and status of the natural vegetation of these areas. Between the continuous dense forest and the thorn scrub is a mosaic of forest of varying height (with a greater or smaller proportion of deciduous and evergreen trees) alternating with savannas, the tall grasses dotted by small trees. These savannas, which today occupy most of the area, are in part artificial, in part natural, and botanists disagree profoundly as to the relative importance of these two groups. This uncertainty is of great concern to geomorphologists, particularly as we have taken as the basis of the classification of our erosion systems the state of the natural vegetation. A reasonable position to take is to suggest that natural savannas are extensive over wide areas as a function of the edaphic conditions. Within this general scheme, very varied combinations may occur, between the following extremes:

(a) The steep slopes are wooded, while vast intervening plains are occupied by savanna. This is because they are inundated from time to time during the rainy season (as a result of their poor drainage) and are dry during the other seasons, and also because the texture of the soil is finer, and so favourable to grasses.

(b) Large plateaus are covered by savanna because their ancient soils have been leached of their fertile elements. The steep slopes that occur beneath these plateaus have young soils and are covered by forest. These forests also extend along the valley at the foot of these slopes wherever this is followed by a large river of sufficient gradient.

It is a corollary of these considerations that the plant cover can change during the course of a cycle of erosion, as the slopes change their form and as the soils evolve. Changes of climate can have revolutionary and permanent consequences. For example, a plateau forest on an impoverished soil can exist if it can live on its own detritus in a closed cycle. But if the forest disappears as a result of an arid phase, it will be replaced by savanna and will not be re-established even if the precipitation later returns to its original level. Weak tectonic movements may, for example, decrease the slope of rivers and so disrupt the vegetation, replacing forest by savanna in areas made liable to temporary flooding. However, over vast areas there occurs a homogeneous distribution of open forest, with varying undergrowth. This is the vegetation of the Miombo type found on the crystalline erosion surfaces of eastern and southern Africa. Unfortunately no precise studies of the erosional processes found in this bioclimatic milieu seem to exist.

One of the most constant features of this area are the widespread ferruginous crusts that cover immense erosion surfaces. Their origin presents a very difficult problem for both the geomorphologist and the pedologist. It is necessary to establish to what extent they are of pedological or alluvial origin, and how far they are the result of short-term (seasonal) or very long-term changes of humidity.

Climates with seasonal variations

Contrary to the views of Tricart, we believe that savannas offer conditions at least as favourable for sheet erosion and pedimentation as the caatinga. Measurements of solid transport made in Madagascar and in Africa on experimental watersheds suggest considerable weathering of o.2 mm a year. Further the moistness of the steep slopes, which are often partially wooded, enable decomposition to take place more quickly.

If the processes of erosion occurring in each season are considered, it seems that they are favourable to the parallel retreat of slopes, especially where wooded slopes dominate a savanna-covered plain. In these conditions, chemical decomposition is strong on the slopes, even during the dry season, as a result of the persistent action of vegetation. The agents of transport on these slopes behave almost in the same way as in humid-tropical climates (although the soils are likely to be thinner and less subject to landslips). On the savanna occupying the plain, the erosional conditions change. Though the stems of the adjacent grass tussocks may touch, this is not true at their base (nor is it true of the trees). Particularly at the beginning of the rainy season, before the grass stems have grown, raindrops can fall directly on to the soil surface and make it impermeable; further, at this time there are no small annual grasses growing between the perennial tussocks. Sheet-wash is therefore able to work under its optimum conditions. It must be added that bush fires (which can be started by lightning) reduce the protection afforded by decaying organic matter. Under such conditions, wash can carry the fine detritus provided by the slopes across even a very gentle gradient before floods cover the plain. The slopes retreat parallel to themselves as in arid regions, but much more rapidly. It would appear that this would be the ideal environment for the development of inselbergs. Also, the very low gradients of the footslopes mean that the smallest climatic or tectonic perturbation can obstruct the drainage.

Another factor favouring the rapid evolution of the cycle of erosion is that as the climate is very dry, taken as a whole, the rivers are well provided with large material, favouring the incision of the faster flowing streams. However, there seems to be too little of this large detritus to slow down the movement of material across the lower slopes. It tends to lie at the foot of the steeper slopes, where it rots rapidly as a result of the local increase in moisture ('Jessen effect').

When the forested slopes retreat at the expense of a plateau covered by savanna, there will be no change in the vegetation during the progress of the cycle. The situation is exactly the reverse when the depressions are occupied by forest and the vegetation on the slopes is more open. Other things being equal, this is most likely where the dry season is relatively long. The weathering of the steep slopes is then much slower, while the transport of detritus across the gentle slopes is impeded. Under forest, the basal angle at the foot of the steeper slopes is less distinct and is replaced by a broad concavity.

The problem now arises whether in the framework of this climate with two seasons, the ferruginous lateritic crust can develop, consolidating the pediment. It is first important to note that two distinct genetic types may be distinguished:

(a) A pedological crust resulting from the concentration of iron in the upper part of the soil. Sometimes this will overlie lateritic clays developed under forest, where the essential mineral is kaolin; sometimes they lie directly on the parent rock. The first of these two profiles, the more complete, is generally accounted for in the following way. During the wet season, chemical decomposition occurs, giving lateritic clay; during the dry season, iron oxide precipitates irreversibly because of the higher temperature. This process definitely operates in the zone with a fluctuating water table, i.e. in areas which are fairly level. Major fluctuations in the water table are only possible if it is fed by a catchment area of sufficient size.

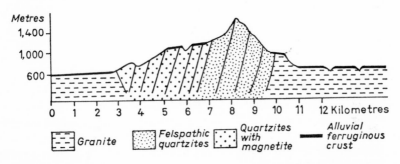

Fig 21   Stepped levels of erosion with an alluvial ferruginous crust on the flanks of Mount Nimba (after Lamotte and Rougerie). The erosion surfaces are perfectly level and protected by the ferruginous crusts derived from the quartzites with magnetite

When the crust lies directly on the fresh rock, this is explained either by the nature of the rock (especially on basic rocks where the transitional zone is always very thin, even under forest, or in quartzites with a high iron content), or it may be due to an appreciably different pedological evolution. In this case the crust represents an illuvial layer resulting from leaching carrying the iron downwards to the contact with the parent rock. It is reasonable to think that this process will be fairly characteristic of a relatively dry climate where the chemical decomposition of the parent rock only just precedes the podsolisation of the upper part of the soil. Whatever the case, the existence of pedological crusts cannot be denied, for they are often closely related to certain rocks, especially basic rocks rich in ferromagnesian minerals (for example on the peridotites of New Caledonia or the gabbros of the Ivory Coast).

(b) Recent research has shown that many of these ferruginous crusts are of a colluvial or even alluvial origin. The following morphological-biological conditions would seem to be the most favourable for their formation. On forested slopes the iron is liberated fairly easily as a result of the abundance of decaying organic matter. When this solution reaches the savannas with their poor drainage, it is precipitated for various reasons: (i) organic matter is less abundant; (ii) the pH rises as a result of the presence in the waters of bases leached from the slopes; (iii) water is evaporated with the onset of the dry season. Sometimes (e.g. Mt Nimba, Venezuela) iron is precipitated on fairly steep slopes of ferruginous quartzitic ridges. Its average free movement is very small because evaporation concentrates the solution after rain.

Alternation of dry and wet climatic phases

Other authors believe, in contrast, that lateritic crusts are formed as a result of a long phase of dry climate succeeding a long humid climatic phase. The pedological problem cannot be separated from the general problem of the morphological evolution. It is from this point of view that the probable consequences of climatic changes will be examined.

The humid phase leads to deep rotting, and clays are formed which may be as much as 100 metres thick, penetrating well below the level of the river beds. This is the phenomenon of crypto-decomposition. This is followed by a dry phase which kills the evergreen forest. On the steeper slopes the clay soil is then readily attacked by wash. The many regions which have recently been cleared of forest help us to see how this stimulates erosion. On the previously decomposed material extremely level pediments develop, similar to those formed on unresistant rocks. Indeed, wash can be likened to the bulldozers that have so easily moved the hills north of Rio de Janeiro. The crystalline cores of resistant rock are exhumed and form inselbergs of durability. In this way an erosional plain is prematurely formed. However, if the climatic crisis is accompanied by incision of the rivers, the regularity of the erosion surface will be disturbed. In fact the valleys, as they are incised, meet cores of hard rock, and are superimposed on these from the soil cover—an example of pedological epigenesis. In these conditions, the erosion surfaces developed in the rotted rock may be broken by masses of resistant rock which escaped crypto-decomposition and so rise above the general base-level. The whole landscape then has a chaotic appearance in relation to the form of the drainage network.

In those areas which were perfectly flat, destruction of the original forest will not lead to any erosion whatever. The increases in surface temperatures will cause the rise by capillarity of ferruginous solutions to form a crust. Thus the hypothesis of climatic variations of large amplitude seems particularly appropriate for the explanation of pedological ferruginous crust when they overlie a horizon of decomposed lateritic clays. The crust will automatically spread over the whole of an erosional surface as it extends by the action of sheet wash.

It should be noted that a result of this evolution is the formation of erosion surfaces that are most extensive where the loss of regolith following the crisis is smallest. The general effect is to perfect the surfaces of erosion normally developed in a tropical-humid climate. The formation of very large inselbergs of the 'Hartling' type thus demands many oscillations through dry and wet phases; for their size shows a total depth of rotting and subsequent soil removal many times the depth achieved in any one such phase, which is likely to be a maximum of about 100 metres. Moreover, as this happens, the cores of durable rock are reduced in size, for at each humid phase they are attacked, however little, by decomposition.

Whatever may be the origin of the erosion surfaces of this area and of their ferruginous crusts, it will be appreciated that these crusts give optimum conditions for the analysis of the polycyclic relief. Thanks to the protective crust (whether pedological or alluvial), the very level surfaces of erosion are perfectly preserved in their original state, even when they have been raised far above base-level. Examples are the Tampoketsa of Madagascar which are fragments of a high plateau capped by an iron crust. As pointed out by Rougerie, the very highest levels are preserved, not as a function of the resistance of the rocks which they cut, but as a function of the extent to which these rocks give rise to thick ferruginous crusts. Particularly important in this respect are the basic rocks, for example the peridotite of New Caledonia. This is also true of minor cyclic flats. Whereas in other climates the old slopes or the old bed of the talweg they represent have undergone subsequent lowering which may well reach several tens of metres, those which are protected by a ferruginous crust on the flanks of Mount Nimba enable the precise reconstruction of the old talweg. The preservation of multiple cycles of erosion is made even easier by the fact that the iron migrates from the higher levels to the lower and is there immediately fixed. Thus even epicycles resulting from brief periods of stability leave some trace.

8 The cycle of erosion in a periglacial climate

The system of erosion can be defined in a simple way: ice is the essential factor in its evolution. Ice is the main factor in the break up of the rock, in the transport of detritus on the slopes, and even in linear erosion, which in turn it paralyses, sets free, and reinforces. In the strict sense, the periglacial area is defined as the area beyond the tree line where the vegetation is discontinuous. But it is obvious that there is also an extensive transition zone where ice is important.

At first sight, periglacial topography is quite distinctive in detail: rocky cliffs covered with talus which often end in smooth footslopes; plateaus on which the soil is decorated by patterned ground; large, poorly-drained plains where rivers meander freely, dotted with curious ridges and small, circular depressions. However, from the point of view of the cycle of erosion, a clear distinction must be made. Many of these forms, in fact, do not play a very important role, either in the evolution of the slopes or in the evolution of the periglacial cycle. They are little more than decorations, certainly characteristic of this system of erosion, but without any morphological effect beyond the scale of tens or hundreds of metres. This is true, for example, of soil polygons, which, because they are developed on gentle slopes, are not accompanied by any notable movement of material. In the same way, pingos evolve *in situ*, especially in alluvial plains. Ice formed in a lens of alluvium draws water from neighbouring areas and the crystal grows. In this way a peculiar abscess is formed, with the soil raised and showing stony fragments; an abscess which finally bursts, and the pingo ends in the formation of a circular lake, like the thousands of examples which cover the plains of Canada and Siberia. But here we will be concerned with large-scale phenomena or with those whose interpretation is essential to a theory of a periglacial cycle of erosion.

There is a preliminary difficulty, similar to that encountered in other areas; as a result of the brief part of geological time during which this system of erosion has occurred, a periglacial cycle of erosion has never run its course. Naturally, attention is focussed on those areas where it has lasted longest; these are the areas which were too dry to have been covered completely by the Quaternary ice-sheets: parts of central Siberia, and particularly, a very extensive area in the Yukon valley of Central Alaska. Yet even this period is still very short; we know that the area north of 60° experienced a temperate climate until the end of the Tertiary, and it is only since the Quaternary, certainly no longer than a million years, that the periglacial cycle of erosion has been in progress in interior Alaska. This length of time is too short for any significant planation in areas of resistant rock.

Everywhere else, the periglacial system of erosion only occurs in areas which have been abandoned by Quaternary glaciers within the last few thousand years. Indeed, a large part of our evidence comes from fossil forms (Germany and Poland). In France, the Pleistocene took the form of an alternation of periglacial episodes and interglacial periods with a cold-temperate climate. There also it is clear that apart from rocks which shatter very easily, the periglacial cycle never reached its end; the system of erosion has left its mark on the evolution of the slopes, but the amount of material removed in this way was always very small. Consequently it is only by extrapolation that one can attempt to define a periglacial cycle of erosion.

The disintegration of the rock is essentially the work of ice, congelifraction. This works at very different speeds; it is very effective in schists and certain limestones where the porosity is favourable: a single winter is sometimes enough to shatter a large block of chalk. By contrast, it is relatively inefficient in attacking massive limestones, many sandstones, and massive crystalline rocks such as granites (Tricart). The explanation of this unequal behaviour poses a very difficult problem. It appears that the pores, where the crystal of ice is formed and grows, have an optimum size. Where the pores are too small, as in the case of granite, a decrease of temperature even to −20°C. will not cause freezing (J. Malaurie). On the other hand, as in many sandstones, the pores may be too large and the water moves too easily during the freezing process; it is important that the water should be trapped and not able to escape as the ice crystal grows. This is the explanation suggested by the following experiment made by constructional engineers to evaluate the resistance of rocks to ice. If a slab of sandstone or limestone is taken, and if the temperature is lowered after it has been plunged in water, the rock remains intact.

If the same slab is then taken and covered with an impermeable substance on all its faces, except that exposed to frost, the slab will break up easily.

Chemical decomposition is evidently less active than in mid-latitudes. However, it is not completely ineffective. In particular, limestone is readily dissolved in cold water provided it is wet for a sufficiently long time. Studies by Corbel have shown that optimum limestone solution occurs in this zone. Limestone is dissolved in large quantities by the melt-water from snow in Spring; this is 20 times richer in carbon dioxide than ordinary water. The other factor which may be responsible for fairly active chemical weathering is the acidity of the bogs. Vegetation decomposes very slowly in the water or saturated soil, giving organic acids. These include the complex range of humic acids, so little studied by chemists; some early experiments have shown that these will attack the iron in crystalline rocks. To these are added mineral acids; in this way, in the bogs of the Harz in Germany, sulphuric acid has been found in appreciable quantities (7.5 mg/litre) deriving from albumen. By contrast, desilification is very slow, as has been shown by the systematic measurements of G. Rougerie from Scandinavia to the Ivory Coast (1–2 mg silicon per litre in Scandinavia, 6–7 mg from Spain to the Ivory Coast).

Ice remains of prime importance because of the quantity of detritus it provides, especially in closely-jointed rocks. Ice is also important in the transport of material on the slopes, particularly in special forms of creep. In the centre of silty materials soaked with water, lenses of ice develop and slowly grow in size by a process which has been illuminated by the fine experiments of Taber. Each initial crystal increases by drawing water from neighbouring areas, provided that capillary movement is possible. A layer of silt may in this way include 80 per cent of its weight of ice. The resulting expansion of the silty lens will be greater downslope than upslope as a result of the effect of gravity. Differential movement of finer and coarser material also results from displacements of this type, due to the fact that ice does not form in the coarser material which is thus displaced and lifted. The best known and most spectacular aspect of this phenomenon is the pipkrake. Needles of ice which form beneath small stones raise them several centimetres. Stones within the soil also tend to be lifted. Vertical, flat pebbles are moved by neighbouring silty beds as they expand, and when the thaw comes, they do not sink back to their original positions.

Ice works in a multiple fashion in this process. First of all, in most periglacial climates the existence of permafrost at a constant depth from the surface (because it is a function of the speed of penetration of heat into the ground) aids slipping. On the other hand, this permanently frozen horizon prevents the percolation of water into the soil. As a result, whereas in other climates the soil is saturated less readily because the water can escape through joints or underlying permeable rocks, etc., all the water is here contained in a layer which does not usually exceed a metre in depth. When a sharp spring thaw melts the snow, the limit of plasticity, and even of soil liquidity is exceeded. This flow (solifluction)[1] varies in speed according to the rock type. It is in silty soils that the limit of liquidity is first reached. Schists and chalk, which are the two rocks most readily shattered, give precisely this type of silty material. By contrast, sandy soils or sands are less easily moved by solifluction because they require more water to saturate them. Ice will also disrupt the cohesion of the soil aggregates.

The two types of transport, saltation by pipkrakes and solifluction, do not have the same importance in the various subdivisions within the periglacial climate. C. Troll has drawn attention to the distinction between the two main types:

(a) A climate with quasi-daily freezing which does not, however, penetrate very deeply. This is found on the one hand in oceanic high latitude areas (such as Iceland), where the average temperature is too high for there to be frozen ground, and on the other hand, on the high tropical mountains which have been the particular interest of Troll. In this climatic type, where the frozen ground is discontinuous, or completely absent, saltation is the more important process.

(b) By contrast, solifluction occurring at the end of the summer is the chief agent of transport in those continental climates where the sub-soil is perpetually frozen (Siberia, Alaska, etc.).

Wash only plays a minor role, although it is not negligible and depends on the amount of snow melt. At the end of spring, the soil is, in effect, saturated to such an extent that a surface flow can be produced on the slopes (noted in Greenland by Malaurie). Moreover, Y. Guillien considers that very fine sheets of chalky talus (coombe rock) have been spread out at the foot of slopes at the time of the last cold phase by wash. This conclusion is drawn from a study of the texture of the material.

[1] The French term *solifluction*, used for all types of flow, has acquired the special usage in English of flow under periglacial conditions of a mass of water, rock and ice. In the rest of this chapter, the term solifluction, rather than flow, will be used [Translators' note.]

In comparison with what happens under temperate or tropical-humid climates, vegetation does not form an inhibiting factor in the movement of detritus. Quite the reverse: the effectiveness of frost shattering and solifluction often determine the density of the vegetation. Where solifluction is active, only a few specialised plants can exist, hanging on with the aid of roots that grow downslope several metres each year (*Dryas* in Spitzbergen). On schistose rocks there are often true biological deserts by virtue of the rapidity of disintegration. It is, then, the most resistant rocks which are the most favourable because plants can survive there; a paradoxical relationship that is the reverse of that found in all other climatic regions.

The true limiting factor on the loss of material from the slopes is water, essential for frost shattering, for solifluction and for creep. Laboratory experiments have only been able to produce rapid disintegration when the samples were thoroughly soaked. It is probable that the progress of erosion is extremely dependent upon the amount of moisture in different periglacial climates. The heaviest precipitation occurs in the north of the Scandinavian peninsula, and measurements made by Hjulström and Rapp have shown that significant losses of material can occur in a few years. The study of mountain slopes on schistose rocks in northern Lapland undertaken by A. Rapp gives some indication of the order of magnitude of the speed of erosion. Mass movements, mainly indicated by mud-flows, represent a loss of 0.03 mm/year, the fall of individual stones about 0.006 mm/year and avalanches 0.01 mm/year. Unfortunately measurements made on the speed of solifluction are not comparable, for they were made on morainic material. All one can conclude is that when the schists are weathered by frost shattering to a material of similar granulometry to the moraine, the regolith is removed at a speed of two cm a year through a thickness of 25 cm.

Similarly, measurements made in the mountainous periglacial conditions of the temperate zone by Cailleux, have shown that a striated soil, intentionally destroyed by those making the experiments, was reformed within two years. The stones in this talus were moved in the proportion of 1:6 over a distance varying between five cm and 4.50 metres. But the first systematic studies of the Spitzbergen slopes which still have a relatively moist periglacial climate, show that the rock cliffs and talus cones evolve slowly; comparison of good photographs taken at an interval of 25 years shows no alteration at all. The point of impact of a falling rock noted on a photograph taken in 1908 is still clearly visible. It is to be supposed that denudation must be extremely slow where the more arid types of the periglacial climate are concerned, for example in northern Canada.

On the other hand, water derived from snow-melt and rain showers does not flow for long enough to excavate first-order talwegs or to remove detritus on slopes of the order of 10° so these are not developed. Movement will occur on slopes steeper than the angle of friction; in this case avalanche channels are incised and pebbles detached by frost will slide across hard snow.

It is probably this feature which is one of the factors responsible for the development of Richter slopes which seem to be a characteristic stage in the evolution of the periglacial cycle (a stage which admittedly is rarely reached in the present arctic area for lack of time). These talus planes reach their maximum development in structures where marls and limestones alternate. Even on silicate rocks, in moderate mountains in the temperate zone which were formerly subject to a periglacial climate, or in Alaska, one finds relatively extensive slopes a few kilometres in length, with many undulations and hummocks that are due entirely to solifluction. These talus slopes are in part due to accumulation and in part to erosion. Their origin implies that the first-order valleys have stable long profiles as a result of the lack of power of linear erosion. They are restricted to the removal of detritus provided by lateral slopes which moves down the line of maximum slope, i.e. obliquely relative to the talweg.

The projections above this talus are worn down by frost shattering (congelifraction) which will come to an end when the detrital cover protects the rock from freeze-thaw alternations.

Fluvial erosion is necessarily limited by the small quantity of run-off; this varies between 200 and 500 mm. But it should be noted that this discharge is concentrated into a small number of months in the summer, so that the capacity of transport may well be of the same order of magnitude as that for a river in the Paris Basin. The considerable amplitude of these seasonal discharges is a favourable factor for lateral erosion, well shown in Canadian aerial photographs of the Mackenzie valley. For those rivers which flow polewards, including those of Siberia, the spring break-up first occurs upstream and large volumes of water flow over a frozen bed. They are thus able to attack only the banks, which is a favourable factor for the development of large surfaces of lateral planation which extend at the expense of the superficial, unfrozen layer. The capacity of these late-spring floods is considerable, as is their competence, for large blocks are rafted along on the ice. Finally, regressive erosion attacking hard rocks has been considerably aided by frost-shattering at the bottom of the bed where water is readily available. There seems to be no reason to deny periglacial streams a considerable erosional potential, at least in the humid phases of this climate.

However, not all periglacial slopes show this regularity. Quite the reverse, for some are scarred by multiple microflats, or *goletz*. These are low banks, a few metres in width, with the upper part cut into the solid rock while the lower part consists of an accumulation of colluvial material brought down by solifluction. It appears that this involves the exaggeration of small initial irregularities in the profile of the slope, irregularities which are exaggerated by the effects of nivation beneath snow banks.

What eventually happens to the constant slopes? Some authors believe that they are capable of parallel retreat. In much the same way, E. de Vaumas believes that gentle pediments on soft rocks form under periglacial conditions, solifluction removing any material which falls down from the free face. In the absence of an adequate period of stability, the study of the Arctic zone does not give us a direct answer. However, a priori considerations lead us to think that successive profiles will develop increasingly greater concave curvature, with an ever gentler average slope. In effect, the equilibrium slope of the dry material is capable of being modified progressively by flow. Frost action will produce increasingly fine material which will become soaked with water: the proportion of this finer matrix and its degree of wetting will both increase progressively downslope.

Surfaces of equiplanation or of altiplanation have often been noted as intimately related to the evolution of the periglacial cycle. They involve the formation of surfaces, partly cut in rock, partly built up by deposition; the filling up of large valleys and the retreat of the slopes on each side. An evolution of this type can only result from a break in equilibrium which is probably climatic. There would seem to be no reason why the streams should pass through a régime of incision followed by a régime of deposition if the load/discharge ratio has not been significantly affected. It is true that it might be anticipated that in the youthful stage of the cycle the talwegs are incised rapidly because the steep rock slopes do not disintegrate in the absence of water. However, it should be noted that at least under the humid form of the periglacial climate, this paralysis does not occur. Snow accumulates more readily than running water in arid climates, and in the supraglacial Alpine area, frost breaks up the rocky arêtes at great speed. Even in drier climates, it does not, in principle, seem likely that the diminution of slope following the end of incision would lead in turn to such an increase in the rate of rock disintegration *in situ* that the load carried by the slopes exceeds the transporting capacity of the river. The more the slope diminishes, the more the average size of the detritus decreases, and the overloading of a river is determined much more by the calibre of the load than by its total amount. The hypothesis that there exists an optimum angle of slope intermediate between the steepest and the most gentle slopes, providing a maximum load for the river, appears doubtful. In any case, beyond this optimum, the river would begin to incise again.

The phenomena of contemporary deposition noted from periglacial areas are more simply explained either by tectonic movements (upwarping of the mouths of the Siberian rivers), or more generally by the substitution of the periglacial system of erosion for the glacial system which had eroded enormous basins. This is particularly the case in Spitzbergen. The talus itself, wherever it is thick, is to be considered, not as a normal feature of the periglacial cycle, but as the beginning of the alteration of the rocky slopes cut by the glaciers. In more general terms, talus the whole world over is the result of climatic or tectonic disturbance.

Conclusion

The whole problem of the evolution of the cycle of erosion in different climates is dominated by the conflict between peneplanation and pediplanation which gives rise to passionate controversy. Whatever may be the solution reached in any particular case, certain essential logical principles must not be forgotten. The most important is that a steep slope can only retreat parallel to itself, preserving at the same time its angle and its approximate size, if the detritus which it provides can be moved across a gentle slope; this can depend both on the agent of transport and the fineness of the colluvial material. The first of these two factors predominates in a hot and dry climate, and the second in a hot and wet climate. But although both types of evolution lead to the juxtaposition of steep residual relief and areas which have been prematurely levelled, the morphology of these level surfaces is very different in the two types of tropical climate which we have distinguished. True pediments, examples of particularly precocious levelling, imply that the small talwegs have no erosional advantage in relation to the open slopes, a relationship only found where plant cover is discontinuous. Under a continuous vegetation cover, by contrast, the talweg incises itself into the decomposed rock, and a system of slopes is formed which gradually declines towards a level surface.

In temperate climates, where the weathering of large blocks is slow, but where their comminution and their incorporation in a fine matrix allows their movement on slopes of varying degree, the cycle of erosion evolves towards peneplanation. The concave slope always remains gentle, each section just being able to evacuate the material received from the next section upslope; this material always includes a certain proportion of large detritus. It is probable that at least in rocks which have not been severely frost-shattered, the periglacial cycle works in the same way.

References

Introduction (pp. 9–12)

BAULIG, H. (1952a) Cycles et climat en géomorphologie, *50ème ann. Laboratoire de Géographie, Rennes*, pp. 215–39
— (1952b) Surfaces d'aplanissement, *Ann. de Géog.*, 61(325, 326), pp. 161–83 and 245–62
— (1955) *Essais de géomorphologie*, Paris
— (1956) Pénéplaines et pédiplaines, *Bull. Soc. Belge Et. Geogr.*, 25(1), pp. 25–58

BIROT, P. (1949) *Essai sur quelques problèmes de morphologie générale*, Lisbon, Inst. Alta Cultura, Centro Estudos Geog.
— (1955) *Les méthodes de la morphologie*, Paris, Presses Universitaires de France (Coll. 'Orbis')
— (1961) Réflexions sur les profils d'équilibre des cours d'eau, *Ztschr. f. Geomorph.*, pp. 1–23, 29–105, 226–45. *Précis de Géographie Générale*, Paris 1965, 2nd ed.

CAILLEUX, A., and J. TRICART (1965) *Introduction à la géomorphologie climatique*, Paris, S.E.D.E.S.

COTTON, C. A. (1942) *Climatic Accidents in Landscape Making*, Christchurch

DÜSSELDORF. GEOGR. VORTRÄGE (1927) Breslau. Collected papers that represent the pioneer work on climatic morphology

Chapter 1 (pp. 14–26)

BIROT, P. (1962) *Contribution à l'étude de la désagrégation des roches*, Paris, C.D.U.

BLACKWELDER, E. (1925) Exfoliation as a result of rock weathering, *Jour. Geol.*, 33(8), pp. 793–806
— (1927) Fire as an agent in rock weathering, *Jour. Geol.*, 35(2), pp. 134–40
— (1933) The insolation hypothesis of rock weathering, *Am. Jour. Sc.*, 26(152), pp. 97–113

CORRENS, C. W. (1951) La descomposición quimica de los silicatos en el laboratorio y en el suelo, *Ann. Edagologia y Fisiologia Vegetal*, 62, pp. 625–636

— and W. VON ENGELHARDT (1938) Neue Untersuchungen über die Verwitterung des Kalifeldspates, *Chemie der Erde*, 12, pp. 1–22

FREDERICKSON, A. F. (1951) Mechanism of weathering, *Bull. Geol. Soc. Am.*, 62(3), pp. 221–32

GENTILLI, J. (1950) Rainfall as a factor in the weathering of granite, *C.R. XVIe Congr. Int. Géog.*, Lisbon, 2, pp. 263–9

GRIGGS, D. T. (1936) The factor of fatigue in rock exfoliation, *Jour. Geol.*, 44(7), pp. 783–96

KVELBERG, I., and B. POPOFF (1937) Die '*Tafoni*' *Verwitterungscheinung*, Latvijas Universitäte, pp. 129–369

PEDRO, G. (1964) *Contribution à l'étude expérimentale de l'altération géochimique des roches cristallines*, Paris, I.N.R.A.

REICHE, P. (1950) *A Survey of Rock Weathering*, Univ. of New Mexico

VORE, G. DE (1956) Surface chemistry as a chemical control on mineral association, *Jour. Geol.*, 64(1), pp. 31–55

Chapter 2 (pp. 27–38)

ACKERMANN, E. (1948) Thixotropie und Fliesseigenschaften feinkörniger Böden, *Geol. Rundschau*, pp. 10–28

SHARPE, C. F. S. (1938), *Landslides and Related Phenomena*, New York

SOUCHEZ, R. (1966) Réflexions sur l'évolution des versants en climat froid, *Rev. Géo. Phys. Géol. Dyn.*, pp. 317–33

TERZAGHI, K., and R. B. PECK (1948) *Soil Mechanics in Engineering Practice*, New York

Chapter 3 (pp. 39–54)

ARNBORG, L. (1953) The sand-trap; an apparatus for direct measurement of bed load transportation in rivers, *Geografiska An.*, 35(2), pp. 75–82

BIROT, P. (1952) Sur le mécanisme des transports solides dans les cours d'eau, *Rev. Géomorph. Dyn.*, 3(3), pp. 105–41

BLACHE, J. (1942) Volume montagneux et érosion fluviale, *Rev. Géog. Alp.*

DANEL, P., R. DURAND and E. CONDIOLIS (1953) Introduction à l'étude de la saltation, *Mem. Soc. Hydrotech. France*, pp. 217–33

EINSTEIN, H. A. (1950) The bed load function for sediment transportation in open channel flows, *U.S. Dept. Agr. Tech. Bull.*, 1026, p. 70

HJULSTRÖM, F. (1935) Studies of morphological activities of rivers, *Geol. Inst. Uppsala Bull.*, 25

JOVANOVIC, P. S. (1940) *Les profils fluviatiles en long*, Paris

LEOPOLD, L. B. and T. MADDOCK JR. (1953) The hydraulic geometry of stream channels and some physiographic implications, *Geol. Surv. Prof. Paper*, 252, Washington

—, M. GORDON WOLMAN and J. MILLER (1964) *Fluvial Processes in Geomorphology*, New York and London

MACKIN, J. H. (1948) Concept of the graded river, *Bull. Geol. Soc. Am.*, 59, pp. 463–512

Part II: Introduction (pp. 56–9)

TRICART, J. (1953) Erosion naturelle et érosion anthropogène à Madagascar, *Rev. Géomorph. Dyn.*, 4(5), pp. 225–30

Chapter 4 (pp. 60–72)

BAKKER, J. P. (1948) Over tectogene en morfogene Getlijktijdigheid bij de jongere Gebergtevorming in West en Midden-Europa in het Kader van denudatieve Altiplanitie, *Natuurwetenschappelijk Tijdschrift*, 30, pp. 3–53
— and J. W. N. LE HEUX (1947) Theory on central rectilinear recession of slopes, *Kon. Ned. AR. Wet.*, 50–3, pp. 95–9, 1073–84, 1154–62, 1364–79

BÜDEL, J. (1937) Eiszeitliche und rezente Verwitterung und Abtragung im ehemals nicht vereisten Teil Mitteleuropas, *Peterm. Geogr. Mitt.*, Ergänzungsh., p. 229

CAILLEUX, A. (1948) Le ruissellement en pays tempéré non montagneux, *An. Géog.*, 57(305), pp. 21–39

DIJK, W. VAN, and J. W. N. LE HEUX (1952) Theory of parallel rectilinear slope recession, *Kon. Ned. AR. Wet.*

SAVIGEAR, R. A. G. (1952) Some observations on slope development in South Wales, *Trans. Inst. Br. Geog.*, 18, pp. 31–51

Chapter 5 (pp. 73–94)

BAKKER, J. P. (1957) Zum Granitverwitterung und Methodik der Inselberg Forschung in Surinam, *Abh. Deutch. Wissenschafttag*, Würzburg

BIROT, P. (1958) *Les dômes cristallins*, Mémoires et Documents du C.N.R.S., VI, Paris

BRAJNIKOV, B. (1953) Les pains de sucre du Brésil, sont-ils enracinés?, *C.R. Som. Soc. Géol. France*, p. 267

FREISE, F. W. (1932) Erscheinungen des Erdfliessens im Tropenurwalde, *Ztschr. f. Geomorph.*, 9, pp. 85–98

— (1933) Brasilianische Zuckerhutberge, *Ztschr. f. Geomorph.*, 8(2), pp. 49–66
— (1936) Bodenverkrüstungen in Brasilien, *Ztschr. f. Geomorph.*, 9(6), pp. 233–48

HENIN, S., and S. CAILLIERE (1952) Sur l'évolution de la phlogopite à Madagascar, *C.R. Cong. Géol.*, Algiers, 18, p. 57

MARTONNE, EMM. DE (1940) Problèmes morphologiques du Brésil Tropical Atlantique, *An. Géog.*, 49(277), pp. 1–27, and 49(279), pp. 106–29

RUELLAN, F. (1931) La décomposition et la désagregation du granite à biotite au Japon et en Corée, et les formes du modelé qui en résultent, *C.R. Congr. Int. Géog.*, Paris, 2, pp. 670–83
— (1940) *Le Kwansai*, Tours

SAPPER (1935) Géomorphologie der feuchten Tropen, *Geog. Schriften*, ed. A. Hettner, Leipzig

TRICART, J., and A. CAILLEUX (1965) *Le modelé des régions chaudes*, Paris, S.E.D.E.S.

WENTWORTH, C. K. (1928) Principles of stream erosion in Hawaii, *Jour. Geol.*, 36(5), pp. 385–419
— (1943) Soil avalanches in Oahu (Hawaii), *Bull. Geol. Soc. Am.*, 54(1), pp. 53–64

WHITE, L. S. (1949) Process of erosion on steep slopes of Oahu (Hawaii), *Am. Journ. Sc.*, 247(3), pp. 168–86

Chapter 6 (pp. 95–117)

BERKEY and MORISS (1942) *Geology of Mongolia*

BIROT, P. (1949) Sur le problème de l'origine des pediments, *C.R. XVIe Congr. Int. Géog.*, Lisbon, 2, pp. 9–15
— (1951) Sur les reliefs granitiques en climat sec, *Bull. AGF*, 220/1, pp. 138–41
—, R. CAPOT-REY and J. DRESCH (1956) Recherches morphologiques dans le Sahara Central, *Trav. Inst. Recherches Sahariennes*, p. 74
— and J. DRESCH (1966) Pediments et glacis dans l'Ouest des U.S.A., *An. Géog.*, pp. 513–51
— and F. JOLY (1952) Observations sur les glacis d'érosion et les reliefs granitiques au Maroc, *Mém. et Doc. C.N.R.S. Centre de docum. cartogr. et geogr.*, 3, pp. 7–56

CAILLEUX, A. (1950) Ecoulements liquides en nappe et aplanissements, *Rev. Géomorph. Dyn.*, 6, pp. 243–70

DAVIS, W. M. (1933), Granitic domes of the Mohave desert, *Trans. San Diego Soc. Nat. Hist.*
— (1938) Sheetfloods and streamfloods, *Bull. Geol. Soc. Am.*, 49(9), pp. 1337–416

DRESCH, J. (1949) Sur les pédiments en Afrique méditerranéenne et tropicale, *C.R. XVIe Cong. Int. Géogr.*, Lisbon, 2, pp. 19–28

— (1955) Critique à BIROT, P. et JOLY, F. (1952) *Rev. Géomorph. Dyn.*

FAIR, T. J. D. (1948) Hillslopes and pediments of the semi-arid Karoo, *S. Afr. Geogr. Journ.*, 31, pp. 71–9

JOLY, F. (1953) Quelques phénomènes d'écoulement sur la bordure du Sahara, dans les confins algéro-marocains et leurs conséquences morphologiques, *C.R. Cong. Int. Géol.*, Algiers, 7, pp. 135–46

MARBUTT, J. (1952) A study of granite relief from South-West Africa, *Geol. Magazine*, 89(2), pp. 87–96

Chapter 7 (pp. 118–24)

BIROT, P. (1963) Contribution à l'étude géomorphologique des plateaux du Centre de Madagascar, *Rev. de Géogr. de Madagascar*, 3

BÜDEL, J. (1957) Die doppelten Einebnungflächer in den feuchten Tropen, *Ztschr. f. Geomorph.*, pp. 201–28

DAVEAU, S., M. LAMOTTE and G. ROUGERIE (1962) Cuirasses et chaînes birrimiennes en Haute Volta, *An. Géog.*, pp. 460–82

DRESCH, J. (1956), Les surfaces d'aplanissement et les reliefs résiduels sur le socle cristallin, en Afrique Tropicale, XVIIIe Congr. Int. Géog. Rio de Janeiro, *Résumés des Communications*, 29

KING, L. C. (1948) A theory of bornhardts, *Geog. Jour.*, 112, pp. 83–7

KREBS, N. (1942) Über Weren und Verbreitung der tropischen Inselberge, *Abbd. Preuss. Akad. Wiss.*, Math-Natur. Klasse, 6

LAMOTTE, M., and G. ROUGERIE (1953) Les cuirasses ferrugineuses allochtones. Signification paleo-climatique et rapports avec la végétation, *Conf. des Africanistes de l'Ouest*, Abidjan, 1, p. 89

LECLERC, J. C., J. RICHARD-LOLARD, M. LAMOTTE, G. ROUGERIE and R. PORTERES (1955) La Chaîne du Nimbá, essai géographique, *Mém. IFAN*, Dakar, 43

MAIGNIEN, R. (1958) Contribution à l'étude du cuirassement du sol en Guinée Française, *Mém. Serv. Carte Géol. Alsace-Lorraine*

PELISSIER, P., and G. ROUGERIE (1953) Problèmes morphologiques dans le bassin de Siguiti (Haut Niger), *Bull. IFAN*, Dakar, 15(7), pp. 1–47

Chapter 8 (pp. 125–32)

C.N.R.S. (1954) *Quaternaire et Morphologie*, Colloque du C.N.R.S., Lyon

RAPP, A. (1960) Recent development of mountain slopes in Kärkevagge (Northern Scandinavia), *Geogr. Ann.*

TRICART, J. (1951) *Le modelé périglaciaire. Cours de géomorphologie*, 2e partie, fasc. 1, Paris, C.D.U.

— (1956) Étude expérimentale du problème de la gélivation, *Biul. Peryglacjalny*, Lodz, 4, pp. 285–318

TROLL, C. (1944) Strukturböden, Solifluktion und Frostklimate der Erde, *Geol. Rundschau*, 34, pp. 546–672

UNION GEOGRAPHIQUE INTERNATIONALE (1952) *Rapports préliminaires de la Commission de morphologie périglaciaire* pour la VIIe Assemblée Générale et le XVIIIe Congrès International de Géographie (Washington), New York

Index